SHISHIR SRIVASTAVA is a motivational speaker. Current _____
department, Personality Development and Career Counselling,
Montessori School, Lucknow. He and his wife, Sophia, have a seven-
year-old son, Srijan. This is his first book. For more details, visit
www.shishirsrivastava.org.

Praise for *The Eight Powers Within You*

'"Positive" and "powerful" are the two words that I would use to
describe Shishir Srivastava's instinctive new book. Incorporating the
"eight powers" in a person's conduct and character can be a potent
formula for an individual's success in today's competitive world'
—Shashi Tharoor, minister of state for external affairs

'*The Eight Powers Within You* is an eye-opener. It is a must-read for all
those who wish to succeed and make full use of their hidden strength
by mobilising the eight supreme powers that lie within each one of us'
—Cassam Uteem G.C.S.K, president of Mauritius (1992–2002)

'*The Eight Powers Within You* is refreshment for the human spirit.
Shishir Srivastava's book is an empowering guide that leads one to
perceive life as an adventure: the advent of destiny. His eight success
principles, simple and profound, are animated with stories that are
vivid and unforgettable. The book is a masterpiece'
—Marilyn Wilhelm, author of *Education: The Healing Heart*
and founder director, Wilhelm Schole International, USA

'Shishir Srivastava has written a beautiful book to inspire the search
for truth. Through his words, affirmations, visualizations and stories,
he has created a colourful tapestry of inspiration to energize the entire
being'
—Nayaswamis Haridas and Roma Blake, directors, Anand Sangh

'*The Eight Powers Within You* is a truly inspiring book and has many
practical exercises to help an individual become successful'
—R.K. Atri, CEO, Bharat Shodh

The Eight Powers Within You

Your Guide to Success

SHISHIR SRIVASTAVA

PENGUIN BOOKS

PENGUIN BOOKS
Published by the Penguin Group
Penguin Books India Pvt. Ltd, 11 Community Centre, Panchsheel Park,
New Delhi 110 017, India
Penguin Group (USA) Inc., 375 Hudson Street, New York, New York 10014,
USA
Penguin Group (Canada), 90 Eglinton Avenue East, Suite 700, Toronto,
Ontario, M4P 2Y3, Canada (a division of Pearson Penguin Canada Inc.)
Penguin Books Ltd, 80 Strand, London WC2R 0RL, England
Penguin Ireland, 25 St Stephen's Green, Dublin 2, Ireland (a division of
Penguin Books Ltd)
Penguin Group (Australia), 250 Camberwell Road, Camberwell, Victoria
3124, Australia (a division of Pearson Australia Group Pty Ltd)
Penguin Group (NZ), 67 Apollo Drive, Rosedale, North Shore 0632,
New Zealand (a division of Pearson New Zealand Ltd)
Penguin Group (South Africa) (Pty) Ltd, 24 Sturdee Avenue, Rosebank,
Johannesburg 2196, South Africa

Penguin Books Ltd, Registered Offices: 80 Strand, London WC2R 0RL, England

First published by Penguin Books India 2010

ISBN 9780143414117

Typeset in Sabon by Eleven Arts
Printed at Manipal Press Ltd, Manipal

Contents

Acknowledgements

My special thanks to:

Dr Jagdish Gandhi, who borrowed Rs 300 from a neighbour in 1959 and started a school with five pupils to impart value-based education and nurture world citizens. Today, City Montessori School, Lucknow, has over 37,000 students. The *Guinness Book of World Records* recognizes it as the world's largest school in a single city. Dr Gandhi has also shown the path to success and achievement to innumerable people. His key message: work hard to serve others.

Sophia, my wife, who inspired me to write this book and without whose constant support and encouragement this would not have been possible.

Heather Adams, my editor at Penguin. Her ideas made this book better.

All my friends and colleagues who have been a source of inspiration throughout my writing.

You, for picking up this book.

Introduction

Let a new race of spiritual beings evolve!
Let a new world civilization prevail!

THE EAGLE WHO GREW UP WITH CROWS

There is a story about an eagle who laid an egg in a crow's nest. The baby eagle grew up with the crow's family, thinking that he too was a crow. One day, the eagle's mother visited her baby. She introduced herself and told him that he was not a crow but an eagle, and was meant to soar high in the sky. But the baby eagle refused to believe his mother.

A few months later the crow told her brood that it was time to fly. All the young birds made an attempt to fly. The baby eagle noticed that his feathers were far bigger than those of his siblings. So he tried to fly higher and higher—and succeeded. The mother eagle was circling above and noticed him. She dived down and joined him. The baby eagle realized that he had been wrong. He decided to leave the crow family and join his real family.

THE BABY EAGLE AND US

Many times we too behave like this baby eagle. Although we have all the powers, strength and resources at hand, we are unwilling to venture forth boldly—either because we are not aware of our powers or are afraid of using them.

That you have picked up this book shows you are keen to know about the 'eight powers within you' and want to lead a successful life. This book is meant for you. It has a message for everyone who is seeking success. It will offer hope to those who are struggling to fulfil their dreams. It will also prove useful to those seeking to make little improvements in their life.

AN IMPORTANT NUMBER

Why 'eight' powers? Well, '8' is a wonderful symbol: if turned by 90 degrees, it becomes ∞ (infinity). So, '8' symbolizes infinity, and that is the magic of the eight powers within you. Turn them around and you will see infinite opportunities. Wealth and happiness will start embracing you.

These powers are available to you right now. The tips given in this book will help you to marshal these powers to work in your interest as well as that of all humanity.

The eight powers are lying suppressed within you. When you decide to use all of them, employing the step-by-step process mentioned in this book, they will awaken. All the powers are interconnected: once you start nuturing one, the others too will begin developing gradually.

The sky is the limit to which any individual can expand any power, regardless of their current position. You can develop each one of the eight powers to any extent you wish.

If your motive is good, your intention is pure and you work for the benefit of all, the eight powers will act together in harmony and flourish.

BEHIND THIS BOOK

This book started with my quest for self-improvement. Like most people, I used to think that success is a matter of destiny and hard work. But after reading several books on success and self-improvement over 10 years—and tasting a few triumphs myself—I realized that a person's destiny is entirely in their hands.

I conceptualized this book about five years ago, using real-life experiences and knowledge gained through self-growth.

When I started writing, I asked myself, *Is there a systematic process to success? How can average people become extraordinary performers? How can this book be of use to them? What tips can be included to make it a success manual that can be handy in day-to-day life?*

I also asked myself, *What is the relation between me, the world and the universe? What is the role of destiny in shaping one's future?*

These questions encouraged me to explore the deeper meaning of success and spirituality in our life.

After all the study and research, I came to the conclusion that all of us can become more successful than we are now. I also realized that there must exist something readily accessible that can help us expand our possibilities. Throughout my prayers and meditations, I kept asking myself, *'What is it that is common to all human beings and can help us succeed at personal, financial and spiritual levels?'* Gradually I found the answer and discovered the eight powers within—which I believe are common to all humans.

While exploring the field of self-growth and motivation, I found that success and successful people have some things in common. These are:

1) Success is all-inclusive

Most people wrongly believe that success depends on hard work alone. Working hard is essential but it is not enough on its own. No one factor can ensure success. One needs many

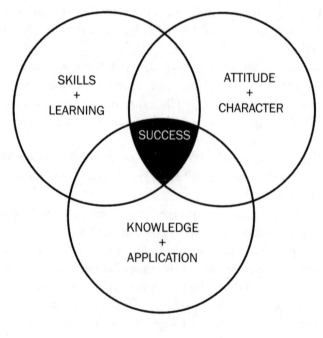

FIGURE A

qualities to be truly successful and most of these are acquired. As a person grows, he learns through experience and experiments. **See Figure A**

2) Successful people use positive energy to their advantage

I found that successful people work with great energy in lesser time and this gives them the power to achieve more. I understood that the entire universe can be broadly classified into two energy fields—positive and negative—and our mind acts as a spiritual broadcasting and receiving centre. When you send out positive energy—through positive thoughts, words or actions—you attract positive things and events in your life. Similarly, negative energy results in negative outcomes. It is like throwing a ball against a wall: it returns to you with equal force. Let's assume this ball symbolizes your emotions and the wall denotes the universe. Now, you have the option to choose your state of emotion—positive or negative—before you throw the ball against the wall. If you write 'love' on the ball and throw it, love will come back to you with equal force. 'Hate' will return as hate. Remember, what you choose to send out is very important. **See Figure B**

3) Successful people know what they want

Successful people *know what they want* and *they go after it until they get it.* They do not lose sight of their aim. They focus all their attention on it. They train their mind to constantly think about accomplishing what they want. And they make persistent efforts. These people organize their lives around this thought, '*I know clearly what I*

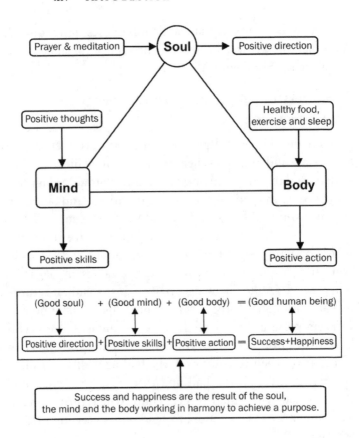

FIGURE B

want and I will keep working hard and long, on myself as well as on the situation, till I get the desired result.' This thought becomes their belief system. It gets stamped on their personality. They turn all their attention towards their goal. It is like a tiger identifying just one prey in the herd, locking its eye on it and chasing it—till the target gives up. **See Figure C**

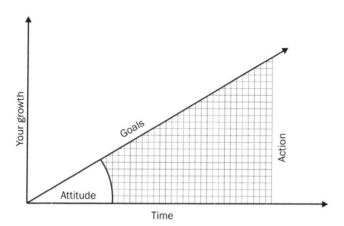

FIGURE C

4) Success has an order

Many people have the wrong notion that success is achieved by chance or destiny and luck plays an important part in life. Each one of us experiences failures and successes. Those who have succeeded have done so because they kept working hard all through the process of learning, unlearning and relearning till the desired results were achieved.

5) Success is possible for anyone

Contrary to popular belief, success is not a privilege of the few. Although many people look for success, only a few pursue their goals with sustained enthusiasm. Anyone who does so can become successful. Unfortunately, not many people keep going till the end of the journey; they often give up before tasting success. **See Figure D**

FIGURE D

HELP IS AT HAND

This book will help you discover ways to empower yourself, to achieve what you desire. Let me say it more simply: this book will create miracles in your life if you work on unlocking the eight powers within you. Remember, it all depends on you—because you are the most important element in choosing, shaping and realizing your destiny.

Here is how to use this book:

1. *Make a journal.* I request you to make the most of this book. You may like to prepare a self-improvement journal before you start reading. You may write down the tips given and apply them in your daily life. You can take

notes and add positive thoughts to your collection. If you maintain a notebook sincerely, you will have put together an entire manual for yourself by the time you finish reading this book. And the manual can serve as your lifelong companion.

2. *Use the tips in daily life.* Each chapter carries empowering questions and beliefs to help readers introspect. You may write these beliefs and questions in a pocket-sized notebook or on index cards, carry them with yourself, and read them often. Before long, you will develop a positive belief system and be able to do what you read about in this book.

3. *Treat this book as a self-empowering course.* Use a highlighter or a pencil to mark what appeals to you. Also treat this book as a manual for self-empowerment and success. Return to it to understand how the eight powers within you work. Then try to develop these powers.

4. *Take time to read this book.* You may finish this book in one go, but I would not recommend that. Read it at your ease to assimilate the tips given here. And why not dedicate one week to practising each power? This way you will learn how to apply these eight powers in just eight weeks.

5. *Practise with enthusiasm.* A driving desire to learn more and practise more to achieve more is required from the start. After reading each chapter, try your hand at the exercises given. Don't wait for 'perfect conditions' to start on them. The only perfect condition is 'now' because this is the only moment you have. Start a working group with your friends if you want. Read and reread the empowering questions and affirmations given towards the end of each chapter. You may use a computer to

record these questions and affirmations, and listen to them over and over again on an iPod. This will help you to assimilate the instructions.

6. *Review.* After you finish reading this book, review it every month—or every week if possible—to get a better understanding of the eight success principles explained here.

A BRIGHT FUTURE AWAITS YOU

'No one can go back and make a brand-new start but anyone can start now and make a brand-new ending.'
—Anonymous

The road to a bright and successful future lies within your reach. God will guide and help you half the way—but only in the second half. For the first half, you will have to walk.

In the following chapters, you will be called to challenge, test, awaken and practise the eight powers within you. And you can start from wherever you are.

I am reminded of some lines from the poem 'Start Where You Stand' by Berton Braley:

'Start where you stand and never mind the past,
The past won't help you in beginning new
The world won't care about your old defeats
If you can start anew and win success;
The future is your time, and time is fleet
And there is much of work and strain and stress;
Forget the buried woes and dead despairs,
Here is a brand-new trial right at hand,
The future is for him who does and dares,
Start where you stand.'

This book will also provide examples of people who have made a remarkable difference to our world by demonstrating their powers. They have used one, two or perhaps all the eight powers mentioned here. I hope the examples will help you relate to these people. You will then discover how you too can contribute to the world.

There are no limits to what you can accomplish; the only limits are the ones you set in your mind. A great adventure is about to begin. Take the first step and start it.

'A journey of a thousand miles begins with a single step.'
—**Confucius**

Prologue: On the Road to Success

'I am the master of my fate; I am the captain of my soul.'

—William E. Henley

THE VOICE WITHIN: YOUR 'SUCCESS SOFTWARE'

Five years ago I was just another person doing an eight-hour job. Nothing noteworthy was happening in my life. I kept longing for something significant to turn up. Months passed, but nothing exciting occurred. I read a lot of self-help books and trawled through self-improvement websites. A couple of years passed, but still nothing new took place. I asked myself why things were in limbo and got the answer: 'Because you are just waiting.' I was taken aback and found to my shame that this was true. Chastened, I tried my hands at a few new tasks and soon had some small successes. I was excited. 'This seems to work,' I thought.

But a month later I was back where I had started. I was not getting any more results. Again I asked myself why I was stuck. Back came the answer: 'The new things you tried last month are thirty days old.'

It is true: new things become old. That is why you must try something different every day. You never know what might click. Any attempt to try something new and grow is an investment. Yes, an investment that gives results with dividends, sometimes manifold.

I learnt an important lesson: if one wants drastic changes in one's life, one must try something drastically new.

Now I do new things all the time. Each day I look for fresh opportunities. Earlier I used to turn them down and, despite hearing the knocking, never bothered to open the door. Now I have changed: if I hear a knock, I immediately open the door and let in whatever opportunity has come my way.

Miracles are taking place in my life because I believe in them. I now listen to the voice within and follow it sincerely— the voice I used to ignore because I thought the suggestions would not work. Now I do not worry about the result when I listen to the inner voice. I simply do what it tells me, certain that the outcome, good or bad, will follow in time. Surprisingly, the results have mostly been favourable. I regret that it took me so long to listen to the voice within and follow it. But I am happy that I do so now.

I have now recognized that this inner voice is great 'software'. It is a 'success software' and it is in all of us. We use our brain, thinking it is the software. Wrong. Our brain is only the periphery. The real brain is our inner voice. It is placed inside us even before we come out of the womb. It is very powerful and runs our brain and body. **See Figure P1**

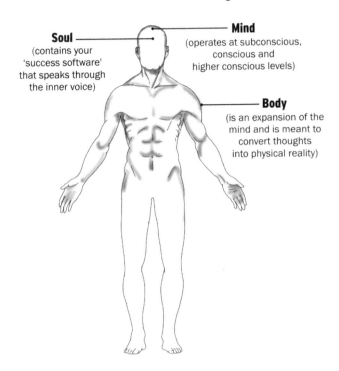

FIGURE P1

The software is in your soul, which holds your destiny. The soul was given to your body because the Creator had a certain purpose to fulfil through you. The soul does not have a tongue but it does have a voice—the inner voice—that we keep hearing. We either suppress it, consciously or unconsciously, or act according to it.

Your success software runs repeatedly, in the form of an inner voice, till you follow its instructions and achieve your goals. Listen to yourself now. Listen, just listen. Spend a few quiet moments with yourself and you will get the answer.

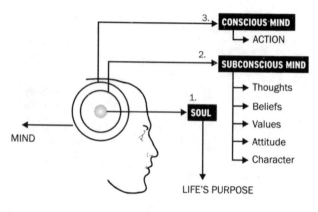

FIGURE P2

Follow the inner voice blindly; you don't need eyes to see it. Follow it 'deafly'; you do not need ears to hear it. Yes, blindly and deafly. Because your eyes can 'see' but they lack a clear vision and your ears can 'hear' but cannot comprehend the eternal voice that has been echoing since the very origin of the universe. You have an inbuilt vision and listening capacity. Use it, use it NOW. **See Figure P2**

TWO CYCLES THAT SHAPE OUR FUTURE

The 'Cycle of Fate' may be strong, but the good news is that there is another cycle too. Known as the 'Cycle of Desire', it is based on human desire. We have the power to create our own cycle of desire. You can mould your destiny in the shape you like and attain the results you want. But the human cycle of desire must run parallel to and in consonance with the cycle of fate. Otherwise it will be crushed. You must decide if your desire to achieve your goal is in harmony with the will of the Supreme Being. If yes, follow it; if not, drop it. **See Figure P3**

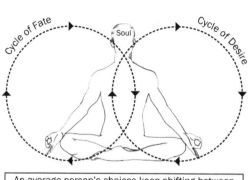

An average person's choices keep shifting between the Cycle of Fate and the Cycle of Desire.

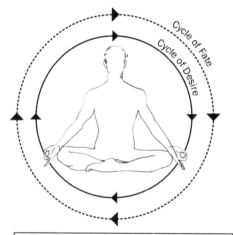

A successful person aligns his choices with both the Cycle of Desire and the Cycle of Fate.

FIGURE P3

If your mind remains in harmony with the universe around it, you can achieve any goal you set. Today, most people are trying to achieve their goals with an agitated mind. This is plain wrong. The mind is a highly sensitive and energetic part of the body. The more you excite and agitate it, the more volatile it becomes. You must keep it calm.

Instead, try to excite your heart and become enthusiastic about the present, the moment you are living in, and about your goal. This will keep stress under control and improve your focus.

During the long process of self-discovery, I came across Eight Universal Truths.

Eight Universal Truths for the universe outside and the universe within:

1. The universe is ever expanding, extremely creative and infinitely energetic, yet perfectly balanced. *Inherently, so are you.*

2. What happens 'in' you affects the universe just like it affects you, but what happens in the universe will not affect you until you allow it to do so. *You should remain aware of the present happenings and how they affect you, and of the choices that you make based upon them.*

3. The universal energy flows in a cyclic way and in two directions: positive and negative. On the whole, it is cosmically neutral and at peace with itself. The positive flow uplifts you; the negative flow pulls you down. *So to be successful, attune your thoughts to the positive flow.* **See Figure P4**

4. What you give to the universe comes back to you with equal force because it travels with the universal energy flow. *Be careful in choosing what you give.*

5. Everything that happens in the universe is only a transformation of energy. What you see as 'creation' is

The Flow of Universal Energy

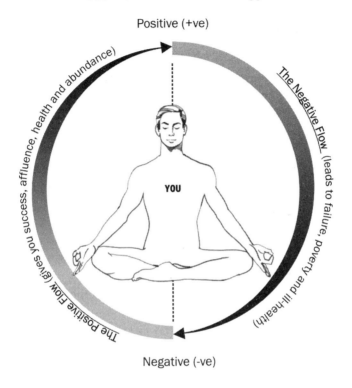

FIGURE P4

actually an 'assembling' of already existing energy. *To realize your destiny, you must transform the infinite energy in you through focused thoughts.*

6. The supreme intelligence is extremely kind and has given you a part of itself to be kind to all that exists. *So, what you want will finally happen if you believe in sharing the riches you earn throughout your journey.*

7. You have to pay a price to accomplish your goals. *This price is not about money; it is usually about work, a change in attitude and giving up old habits or acquiring new ones.*

8. What you see may or may not be true, but what you believe will come about if you hold on to your beliefs. *You will see it happening if you believe in it.*

I do not know what is best for you. Only *you* do. So I urge you to do some soul-searching and explore these ideas. You will find the answer. If not, wait till you read about the eight powers within you and how to develop and apply them.

Happy reading and have a great life.

'Cherish your visions and your dreams as they are the children of your soul, the blueprints of your ultimate accomplishments.'

—Napoleon Hill

One
The Power of Imagination

1. UNDERSTANDING THE POWER OF IMAGINATION

Since childhood I have been taught to believe in the oneness of humanity. In school I dreamt of growing up and working for the good of all.

One day in 2000, I looked at a photograph of the United Nations Headquarters building in a magazine in my office. I then visualized myself standing in front of it. At that time I had no money and no idea how my imagination or desire

1

would take me there. But I kept visualizing my trip to America and reaching the UN till I was convinced that I would be able to do so one day.

Thereafter, I started applying for peace conferences abroad and travel sponsorships. In 2003 I got my first break when I was invited to a seminar on peace education in Hamburg, Germany. Thus began a series of trips to various countries, all sponsored by the organizers. The next year I was asked to attend the Parliament of World Religions in Barcelona, Spain. In 2005, I was invited to a convention at the UN Headquarters. And in July of that year I was finally there in front of the UN building. I also got the chance to share my views in the UN General Assembly Hall.

Aged twenty-nine years, it was a great achievement for me. I was convinced the Power of Imagination did exist in me. I explored it and soon realized it was present in all human beings.

'The source and centre of all man's creative power is his power of making images, or the power of imagination.'

—Robert Collier

What is the Power of Imagination?

Imagination is the creative ability of your mind that helps you form an image of an object or an experience before you bring it to physical reality. The Power of Imagination helps you visualize things that cannot be seen. Simply put, imagination is seeing through mental images. This power is inherent in all of us and can be developed to a very high level. **See Figure 1.1**

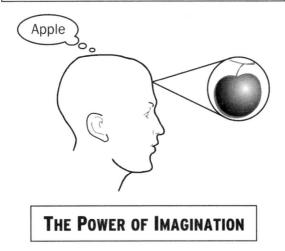

The Power of Imagination helps to project thoughts in the form of images.

Apple

THE POWER OF IMAGINATION

FIGURE 1.1

Great achievements are the result of great imagination

Albert Einstein once said, '*Imagination rules the world.*' Truly it does and Einstein himself proved it. As a sixteen-year-old boy, he imagined what his world would look like if he travelled around the universe at the speed of light. Einstein honed his imagination and ideas for the next nine years, till he shook the world with his special theory of relativity. Scientists have much appreciated Einstein's ability to imagine travelling around the universe and reveal its laws. And he used his Power of Imagination to visualize the result of his discoveries in his mind, not in a physical laboratory.

'When I examine myself and my methods of thought,
I come to the conclusion that the gift of imagination
has meant more to me than my talent for absorbing
positive knowledge.'

—Albert Einstein

If you study the lives of great entrepreneurs, scientists and
inventors, you will find that by using creative visualization
they developed a strong mental picture of what they wanted
to achieve. They used the Power of Imagination to give a
tangible shape to their 'inside picture'. Mahatma Gandhi
visualized achieving independence through non-violent means
and forcing the British to quit India. He succeeded. The Wright
brothers imagined the flying machine and created it even
though they were called 'schizophrenics'. Arthur C. Clarke
conceived that the world would one day be connected through
three satellites; he saw something similar happen during his
lifetime. Edison conceptualized the electric bulb and created
it. Ray Kroc, the founder of McDonald's, visualized establishing
a chain of fast-food restaurants long before he succeeded. All
the great inventions, discoveries and business successes have
been possible only because their originators used the Power
of Imagination to give a clear shape to their ideas on their
'mental screens' before 'bringing them out'. **See Figure 1.2**

The entrepreneur is essentially a visualizer and an
actualizer . . . He can visualize something, and when
he visualizes it he sees exactly how to make it happen.
—Robert L. Schwartz

You too have the Power of Imagination

It is a myth that only a few people possess the Power of
Imagination. Every human has it; you too have this power

These people used their Power of Imagination
and became successful.

MAHATMA GANDHI
Independent India through
non-violence

WRIGHT BROTHERS
Flying machine

ARTHUR C. CLARKE
Satellite

EDISON
Electric bulb

RAY KROC
McDonald's

FIGURE 1.2

within you. It is just that you might not have developed it as much as an Einstein or an Edison. But with perseverance and practice, you can enlarge your Power of Imagination to achieve amazing things.

The Power of Imagination should not be confused with fantasy. Fantasy makes your mind wander in a dreamland, which is good for the growth of your creativity to some extent. But when I say 'imagine', I mean visualizing for a specific purpose.

The power that shapes thoughts into things

Thoughts are energy and you can mould them by using your imagination. Any idea given to the brain time after time settles at the subconscious level—the part of the brain that controls most of our involuntary movements.

Once the subconscious brain accepts any thought or image as reality, it works on it and forces all the body cells to bring that image to reality. It all depends on what kind of image you project on your mental screen.

This is also true about the kind of image you hold about yourself. Psychologists call it 'self-image'. What separates an average individual from an exceptional one is the kind of self-image formed in the mind. If you have an average self-image dominating your brain, you will be among the average lot. If you have an exceptional image about yourself, your brain will help you become an exceptional person. The better your self-image, the better will be your self-esteem and performance.

> *'First comes thought, then organization of that thought into ideas and plans; then transformation of those plans into reality. The beginning, as you will observe, is in your imagination.'*
>
> —Napoleon Hill

The power that can change your reality

Think for a moment: you are what you are today because somewhere in the cycle of time in the past you imagined yourself to be somebody. And here you are. By the same logic, if today you imagine yourself to be somewhere in the future, that is where you will reach. Isn't it amazing? You become what you imagine becoming the most. So, imagine what you want to be in the future and you can reach there, provided you work according to a step-by-step plan using the eight powers within you.

You have the Power of Imagination to change your existing reality. All you need to do is imagine a new set of exceptional images about yourself and keep reminding yourself that you have to achieve your goals. To do this you must have a long-term perspective and project yourself at least five years ahead. Imagine that your life will be perfect in every aspect; hold that image in your mind and start working to attain it. With the Power of Imagination you can imagine in detail what you will become in the future. You can imagine the future 'you' and carry this image within you as you go along. **See Figure 1.3**

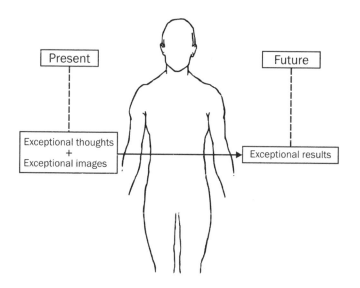

FIGURE 1.3

Change your self-image and your life will change

By reorienting your mental images, you change your belief system. By reorienting your beliefs, you change your expectations about yourself. By reorienting your expectations, you change your attitude. By reorienting your attitude, you change your behavioural patterns. By reorienting your behavioural patterns, you change your performance level. And by reorienting your performance level, you change your life.

All human beings are born to live in abundance and become successful, irrespective of where they live, what education they have had and their background. So are you. But you can start creating a new reality for yourself only when you use the Power of Imagination to redirect your thoughts in a new direction. Think and imagine the future in a positive way and all positive forces will start working in your favour.

> '*If you have built castles in the air, your work need not be lost; that is where they should be. Now put foundations under them.*'
>
> —Henry David Thoreau

2. HOW TO DEVELOP YOUR POWER OF IMAGINATION

The Power of Imagination starts working once you have a clearly defined purpose. You need to focus your mental energy on this purpose to create a detailed image of what you want to achieve. The more clearly you can focus and 'see' what you desire the most, the more your Power of Imagination will work to make it a reality.

Look at any building around you and you will realize that

it was first constructed in a person's imagination. He must have shared his thoughts with an architect who would have then drawn up a map. To make that map a physical reality, the person would have invested faith, energy and resources. Similarly, to achieve your purpose in life and to convert your burning desire into a reality, you must first print out the genetic code of success that lies deep in your mind and soul.

> *'Imagination grows by exercise, and contrary to common belief, is more powerful in the mature than in the young.'*
> —W. Somerset Maugham

Use all five senses to imagine

To speed up the process of making your dreams come true, you need to imagine in vivid detail the reality you want to create. The Power of Imagination helps us to visualize what the eyes cannot see, listen to what the ears cannot hear and feel what the skin cannot touch. You should only think in a positive manner about your desires; otherwise you might trigger situations you do not want to face.

Imagine yourself successful and you will become so; imagine yourself a failure and you will become so. Therefore, you must choose your thoughts carefully, for it is these choices, positive or negative, that will ultimately decide your future. The best way to gain control over your thoughts is to gain control over your feelings. If you have positive feelings and keep negative emotions away, your thoughts will ultimately be positive.

Create a 'vision board'

The actor Akshay Kumar attributes his success to the two posters he stuck up in his dormitory room while he was working as a chef in Thailand. He had a great desire to work with the Hollywood actor Sylvester Stallone and the Bollywood actor Sridevi. So he pasted their posters on the wall facing his bed. The posters were the first things he saw when he woke up in the morning. Gradually, he started believing his dreams would come true. Later Kumar moved to Mumbai to act in films and had some early successes. These were followed by many years of struggle and hard work. Now, 20 years after those days of visualization in Thailand, Kumar's dream of acting with Stallone and Sridevi has been fulfilled.

Creating a 'vision board' helps you to develop your imagination. You can paste pictures of the people you admire and want to be like on a soft board. You can also stick up photographs of things you desire, such as a house, a car or a musical instrument.

You can even paste your own photograph on the board and 'see' yourself living your dream lifestyle, being successful. Place the board where you can see it daily. By creating new images on the screen of your mind, you can attract these things into your life.

Create a mental screen

To visualize any success, you must first calm your mind and create a mental screen. This screen is a blank space where you first visualize yourself doing something before actually doing it. It is a process that can be mastered with daily practice.

Visualization is so powerful because it helps us to organize our thoughts. A few calm moments on the mental screen can energize you and help you move towards your goal. When the energy within you is organized, your world outside gets shaped in the same way.

'The future is simply infinite possibility waiting to happen. What it waits on is human imagination to crystallize its possibility.'

—Leland Kaiser

3. AN EMPOWERING EXERCISE TO UNLEASH THE POWER OF IMAGINATION WITHIN YOU

How to beat stress through the Power of Imagination? Meditate with the moon by practising Yog Nidra

Lie down comfortably in a quiet room. Relax your body and do some deep breathing, five to ten times. Close your eyes and resume normal breathing. Feel that you are one with yourself. Now imagine that a white band of light is shining around your body and covering it.

While you hear your breathing movement, visualize lying near a beach where you can hear the sound of the waves breaking against the shore. Imagine an evening breeze is blowing, the sun is setting, the stars are starting to appear and the moon is shining brightly.

Now imagine getting up slowly. Feel and picture yourself moving out of your body and looking back at yourself lying on the floor, totally relaxed.

Visualize that you are weightless, moving away from your body and flying above the Earth's surface. You are slowly heading towards the moon. The Earth is becoming smaller and smaller as you fly towards the moon through space. You can see the stars twinkling and the sun shining brightly. You are getting closer to the moon.

Once you land on the moon, the symbol of the Power of Imagination, your heart and mind are at peace. While you are sitting relaxed and dreaming about the infinite possibilities available to you, you can see the bright future that lies ahead of you. After spending some time there, relaxing and visualizing, you realize that you now want to return to Earth. So you take a leap and start flying back.

As you return to Earth, you see your body on the ground and want to get inside it quickly. You do so and slowly you wake up to full consciousness.

Benefits: *This exercise will help you beat stress and improve your Power of Imagination. You will realize that the universe outside and inside are the same.*

4. THE POWERFUL SYMBOL OF IMAGINATION

Moon: An emblem of tranquillity and creativity, the moon is chosen as the symbol of imagination. It reflects the positive

The symbol of the Power of Imagination

Moon

FIGURE 1.4

light of the sun. If you look up at the moon, you will be filled with positive thoughts and your mind's creative faculty will be ignited. You will realize that the dark night will end and the bright day will follow soon. **See Figure 1.4**

5. AN EMPOWERING PERSONALITY

How the Power of Imagination empowered Bill Gates to think big and visualize what he wanted to achieve

Bill Gates is chairperson and chief software architect of Microsoft Corporation, the worldwide leader in software services and internet technologies for personal and business computing. He is a multi-billionaire.

Gates was intelligent, imaginative and ambitious even as a child. He was bored at school and his parents were always trying to feed him more information to keep him busy. The turning point of his life came when he first saw a computer. In 1968, the 13-year-old Gates and his friends formed a 'programmers group'. Within a week, he knew more about computers than his teacher at school.

In 1975, Gates dropped out from Harvard after completing his first year of college. He soon formed Microsoft with the vision of having *'a computer on every desk and Microsoft software on every computer'*. Today, this vision seems to have come true. Gates 'saw' millions of computers spread all over the world with Microsoft's software much before it really happened.

The important factors behind Gates's phenomenal rise were his Power of Imagination and continuous hard work.

He believes you can achieve anything if you are hard-working and know how to apply your imagination.

Three important lessons can be learnt from Gates's life:

i. You should discover your true liking as early as possible and develop a drive for excellence in your chosen field.

ii. You should use your Power of Imagination to visualize the future and set goals.

iii. You should work hard to achieve your goals.

Read more about Bill Gates at www.microsoft.com.

6. EIGHT EMPOWERING QUESTIONS

i. Am I visualizing things before doing them?

ii. Do I exercise my Power of Imagination regularly? Can I use it more?

iii. How will this look if I tried doing it differently?

iv. Have I tried to organize my imagination to achieve something worthwhile?

v. What will happen if I employ all my senses to imagine vivid details?

vi. Can I see things on my mental screen before I start working on them?

vii. Am I giving myself enough opportunities of exercising my Power of Imagination before I do a thing?

viii. How clearly can I see my goals being achieved?

7. EIGHT EMPOWERING AFFIRMATIONS

i. I have the ability to visualize every aspect of my success and I easily imagine doing my best.

ii. My 'imagination muscles' are getting stronger every day and great ideas come quickly and easily to me now.

iii. I hold images of success in my mind for long periods and am more focused on my goals.

iv. I enjoy imagining a bright future for myself as I go on achieving my goals.

v. My mental 'success rehearsal' is so real that I can feel it and my images of success are getting clearer.

vi. I enjoy working to make my images of success come true.

vii. I quickly turn any pictures of failure into success and imagine how my successes will make me feel.

viii. I live amid infinite possibilities and can achieve great things.

8. EIGHT TIPS TO DEVELOP YOUR POWER OF IMAGINATION

1) **Create a mental screen.** Find a quiet place and sit in a relaxed manner. Look at your surroundings and then close your eyes. Think of your mind as a film screen that helps you recreate the things you saw just moments earlier. To begin with, repeat this process four or five times a day.

2) **Prepare the mental screen to visualize thoughts as pictures.** As your mental screen becomes strong, you

can visualize things with ease. You can prepare it to play films of past and future events. As you train your mind, you will gradually develop the ability to visualize things even while your eyes are open. Once your mental screen is ready and you are prepared to receive the thoughts circulating in the universe, you'll see them as pictures and moving objects.

3) **Act on your imagination.** Close your eyes and visualize moving your hand. Now open your eyes and move it the way you imagined. You can move it, right! This shows that your mind has the power to control your body parts and also to move them according to your imagination. The essence of this step is imagination followed by action. You can practise this 'imagination-action' exercise with other parts of your body. Gradually, you will develop the power to turn your mental 'creations' into reality.

4) **Visualize positive thoughts, expect positive results.** Imagine you are a ship sailing on rough seas. You will find that things are difficult this way. Now shift your mental screen to another picture: think that you are travelling on a sturdy ship and sailing smoothly. How do you feel? Your mind can visualize a reality: a ship sailing towards its destination. But it can see the same picture in two ways: one of discomfort, the other of comfort. To achieve positive results, you should visualize reaching your goals with ease while the sea of energy around you remains calm and your ship sails steadily. So, to achieve success you must imagine only positive results and make positive imagination-action investments. To expand your positive imagination, you may play soothing music, watch inspirational movies

or surround your room with cheerful images and motivational quotes.

5) **Improve your mental images.** Improvement in any sphere of life is possible when you start improving your mental images. Fill your mind with pictures of the person you want to be, the goals you want to achieve and the life you want to live. Constantly visualize being successful, discuss success with friends and hang pictures related to achievement around you. This will give a fillip to your efforts and help you achieve your goals faster.

6) **Mix faith with imagination.** Faith plays a strong role in keeping your imagination intact. It is important that your positive thoughts are constantly reinforced at the subconscious level. Each negative thought or doubt that might arise should be replaced with a stronger positive thought mixed with faith. With constant practice, you can master the art of getting rid of negative emotions and creating space only for positive ones. Each positive thought that leads you to imagine success must sink in your mind and take the form of action. Continuous action will allow your imagination to become a positive force.

7) **Create new thought patterns through imagination.** It is difficult to change habitual thought patterns—and, therefore, habits. The Power of Imagination can make us think creatively and give rise to new patterns of thoughts. With new thought patterns, you can shape new visions of the future. Try to imagine things beyond the realms of possibility.

8) **Practise daily to improve your imagination.** Each thought that you visualize in the form of an image and

strengthen by using different senses will foster your Power of Imagination. As your imagination expands through regular practice, your level of success will also increase. What people think impossible is just something they cannot imagine. If you can imagine it, you can achieve it. The possibilities are infinite; the only limits are the ones you impose upon yourself.

Success Principle #1:
Use the Power of Imagination

Visualize what you want to achieve and create a strong mental image of your goals. Hold these images till you make them come true.

Two
The Power of Words

1. UNDERSTANDING THE POWER OF WORDS

There was a time when I was down in the dumps. I had lost a job and was paid poorly in my new job. My father was suffering from kidney failure and was on dialysis. A major portion of my salary would go towards his treatment. The future looked bleak. One day, I came across a poster with an inspiring message: 'I am light, I am love, I am harmony, I am peace, I am success, I am happiness, I am prosperous, I have great powers within me.' I hung the poster in front of my bed so I could read it each time I went to sleep and as soon as I got up.

These words had a tremendous impact upon me; in fact they turned out to be life transforming. I started believing in them. Soon my life started to change and I became more confident with each passing day. I realized the Power of Words within me. Since then my life has run in top gear.

What are words?

Words are the powerful means through which you express your thoughts. Each word has a spirit. Once spoken or written, it sets in motion a spiritual phenomenon: either in a creative or a destructive way, corresponding to the intention with which the word is expressed. Words generate a great power when they are mixed with emotions and repeated over time. The repetition of positive words generates creative power and of negative words gives rise to negative power. **See Figure 2.1**

The Power of Words shapes our internal dialogue

The Power of Words has a tremendous influence on our behaviour and actions in daily life. Your belief system is made up of and kept alive through your internal dialogue: the communication that you have with yourself. This self-talk has a great impact on your mind.

Internal communication is at work all day, even while you are sleeping. Your intentions spur the selection of the words you say to yourself. Positive words are chosen in case of a positive intention and destructive words are picked in case of a destructive intention. You first start to feed on words and as they gain power through repetition, they build upon themselves and start to control your thoughts, actions and behaviour. **See Figure 2.2**

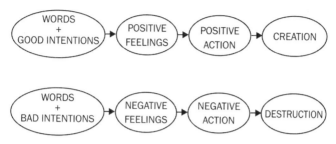

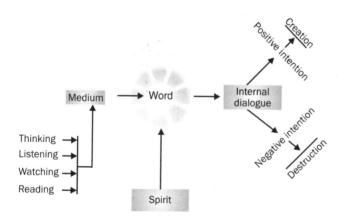

Words reach us through mediums such as thinking, listening, watching and reading. They are shaped by our internal dialogue, which is influenced by our attitude. If words are mixed with positive intentions, they lead to creation; if mixed with negative intentions, they lead to destruction.

FIGURE 2.2

Words can shape your destiny

Your words can shape your destiny and create the kind of life you wish to live. The words that you think, say, write or act upon have a direct role in moulding your road to success. Each word that surrounds your soul, mind and body comes with a spirit that has a powerful influence. Every word that you think, read or act upon has the seed of creation and the potential to grow into the tree of success.

Words have a powerful influence upon us

Listen to a couple of motivational songs and see how you become ready to take action; then listen to some gloomy songs and note how they make you feel low. While a genuine word of appreciation can inspire you to improve your performance, a word of criticism may discourage you. For example, when a child receives constant assurance from his parents that he has the capability to do whatever he wants to, the child keeps on going. If the same child is repeatedly told that he is useless and cannot improve, he feels dejected and may become a pessimist. This is how words influence our behaviour.

> *'Too often we underestimate the power of a touch, a smile, a kind word, a listening ear, an honest compliment or the smallest act of caring, all of which have the potential to turn a life around.'*
> —Leo Buscaglia

In whatever way you choose the words you speak—to yourself or to others—you become an agent of influence. Therefore, you should make your choice of words with care and understanding. Casually chosen words can have a devastating effect and thoughtfully chosen words can create a paradise around us.

2. How to Develop your Power of Words

Words come to us through listening, reading and thinking. The words that we hear in songs and speeches, the ones we read in newspapers, advertisements and books, and those we think and dwell upon the most have a tremendous impact on us. The fourth way by which words reach us is through our inner voice. The words we hear from our childhood on— from our parents, relatives and friends—affect our personality in some way or the other and influence our self-talk. This in turn determines our performance when we grow up.

> *'Guard your speech. Never speak of yourself, your affairs, or of anything else in a discouraged or discouraging way. Never admit the possibility of failure or speak in a way that infers failure as a possibility.'*
> —Wallace D. Wattles

Words can make you or break you

Most people develop a pessimistic attitude towards life because they probably did not get enough words of appreciation, support or encouragement when they were young. Therefore, you must make a conscious effort not to be influenced by negative words even if you hear or read them.

There is a story about three boys who were climbing a tree. The one reaching the top first was to be the winner. From down below, their peers and families kept shouting,

'Don't go up. It's too high. You may fall.' Soon, two boys gave up as they were listening to these negative suggestions. But one boy kept climbing and reached the top. Can you guess why this boy won? Because he had put cotton in his ears and listened only to his inner voice that constantly told him, 'You can reach the top.' Had he listened to the negative words of the people standing around the tree, he too might have given up. But he kept moving up and reached the top.

The moral of the story: you must turn a deaf ear to all the words that arouse fear, insecurity or doubt in your mind. People who say you can't do something are usually those who have either never tried or given up quickly and accepted defeat as a reality.

'Fall seven times, stand up eight.'

—Japanese proverb

Successful people think 'happy words' most of the time

Successful people constantly fill their minds with positive words and images that help them maintain 'sustainable enthusiasm'. They are determined and focused on what they want. They have a plan to follow and act upon it. When they meet failure on the way, which may happen several times, they learn their lesson and continue with new energy towards their goals.

In your daily life, you must listen to the voice within that tells you: 'Yes, I can do it; yes, I can do it; yes, I can do it.' Repeat these five words to yourself whenever you confront a challenging situation. The Power of Words can inspire you to do great things and conquer great heights in life. Words mixed with positive emotions are like what happens during a chemical reaction in the presence of a catalyst. When the catalyst is added, the chemical reaction is further accelerated. Similarly when words are spoken with joy, faith and conviction, they impart power and have an instantaneous impact on the receiver.

Words have the power to move things and people

Great public speakers of the past such as Winston Churchill and Martin Luther King Jr, and present-day motivational speakers such as Anthony Robbins, Zig Ziglar and Brian Tracy have shown how huge groups can be motivated through the Power of Words. If you listen to their speeches, you will find that they add a lot of positive emotions to their words. They speak passionately from their heart to keep audience interest alive. This way their words leave a deep impact on the minds of the listeners. When their speech is over, the audience leaves feeling empowered. It is as if the speaker has, by using words mixed with feelings and emotions, transformed his energy into a great power.

> 'Kind words can be short and easy to speak but their echoes are truly endless.'
>
> —Anonymous

Repetition of words is necessary to generate power

When you try to develop positive qualities through repeated affirmations, you may sometimes feel it is difficult to get rid of the negative emotions that hold you back. It is as if you are trying to jump higher but cannot because your feet are tied up with a rope attached to the ground.

We cannot completely get rid of negative emotions because they act like gravity and pull us down. Just as a small cloud can hide a bright sun, or a grain of coffee can turn white milk into brown, the negative emotions of jealousy, anger, greed, ego or lust can pull us down even when we are performing at our best.

Consider the launch of a spaceship. It takes several years of planning, team building, cooperation, information gathering, material accumulation and engineering to give final shape to the spaceship. Then one day the countdown begins and the rocket is launched. As the spaceship takes off, it has to overcome the tremendous gravity that is pulling it back to Earth. It gradually reaches a level where the Earth's gravity is minimized. Thereafter, it goes up with ease at a constant speed. Similarly, what will take you to stratospheric success are positive words and their constant repetition.

Positive communication through the Power of Words

Positive words have a great power to motivate and bring the best out of a person. In positive communication, words are expressed to invite a productive response, so that the person who hears or receives them takes action. Words chosen without care or concern can damage self-esteem and enthusiasm, whereas words chosen thoughtfully can increase expectations, give hope and inspire a new vision.

Positive communication contains words expressed positively, thereby sending an encouraging message. In this way, the sender first appreciates the work being done by the receiver. The message is composed with the right mindset, so that the receiver takes it up positively. There is no fault-finding, suspicion or malicious intention in positive communication. The sender focuses only on the receiver's good qualities.

The message talks positively of the goal and is expressed in the form of a request. If the receiver is required to do more than one thing, the sender frames the message like a question. This allows the receiver to think, feel involved and take a decision. When the receiver's answer is approved, he feels the job belongs to him. Thus he takes the message positively and starts working to achieve the set goal.

Positive communication creates a belief system which can inspire, influence and instil greatness in us and in others. A positive belief system initiates action leading to creation. The role of words is important, whether you intend to communicate positively with yourself or with others, through writing, speaking or action. When words reach the physical environment through speech and writing, or in the form of symbols, they tend to attract energy.

Thus, positive words gather positive vibes and people around them; and negative words gather negative vibes. Since the power of words is a rare quality bestowed upon humans, you must constantly explore the means to enhance your communication skills—internally, interpersonally and in public.

'The words that enlighten the soul are more precious than jewels.'

—Hazrat Inayat Khan

Speak in a positive way with others

Words have the power to touch people. Thus every word has the potential to motivate someone to achieve great heights. It is like a ripple effect. You communicate your thoughts to a person by words and a ripple is formed from one person to another and from another to the next, and so on.

Always put your head over your heart and think twice before you speak. We usually point out the negative aspects of others without looking at our own shortcomings. Sometimes, even though we intend to correct others, we point out their mistakes without bothering to note their good qualities.

Using words to help a person improve is like making a sandwich. You first put a slice of positive words, then the suggestion you would like to give and finally another slice of positive words. See Figure 2.3

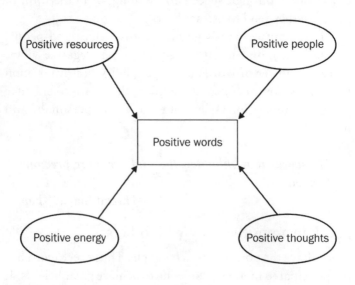

FIGURE 2.3

Keeping a positive attitude helps you to receive words positively

A mind with a positive attitude will receive positive words in a good spirit and will further communicate them to others in the same spirit. The attitude of the person receiving the words and the way they perceive things matter a lot. A person with a negative perception will block positive words and mix in his negative emotions. Result: zero progress. To get ahead, you must think positively and keep your mind open to new ideas and suggestions at all times.

This is why you must give yourself time for introspection and analyze your strengths and weaknesses. This kind of review—from day to day, from week to week and from month to month—allows us to eliminate our weaknesses and build on our strengths.

Honour your words

A good human being is one who always tries to stick to his words. You must think twice whenever you speak or write because a word once spoken is like a bullet that has been fired—it cannot come back. This is a hard fact that none can ever deny. You should make a constant endeavour not to speak ill of others. Your words should be kind and loving, and uttered with care, concern and empathy. Once you generate respect for your words, others will respect you more.

You know that your words can affect other people's thoughts, emotions and behaviour. Sometimes, they can even destroy good relations. You must never take your words lightly. Select them with care and speak them with conviction. At any given moment, you have the power to choose your thoughts and words. The words that you choose with positive faith are powerful and influential. But so are the words chosen with negative intention. You should therefore exercise your choices cautiously. Thoughtfully chosen words are a powerful medium to bring our abstract thoughts into the physical world. This is possible by expressing them appropriately.

Many of us fail to change our attitude because negative forces inside us hold us back. This is one reason why we must give ourselves time for introspection and analyze our strengths and weakness. Such a review enables us to eliminate our weaknesses through our strengths.

3. AN EMPOWERING EXERCISE TO UNLEASH THE POWER OF WORDS WITHIN YOU

Below I am including an exercise which will help you get rid of your negative thoughts and emotions:

Step 1: Visualize that there are two balloons in your mind. A *white balloon* that carries all positive thoughts and words, and a *black balloon* which carries in itself all negative thoughts and words. The white balloon, a light-air balloon, has the potential to take you higher and help you realize your greater self. The black balloon, a heavy-air balloon, has the potential to pull down the white balloon and prevent it from rising.

The white balloon has the potential to fly but it cannot because the heavy air of the black balloon tends to pull it down. The balloons are joined together. Therefore, even when you try to fill in more light air (positive words, emotions) in the white balloon, it does not go any higher because the black balloon (negative words, emotions) pulls it down. **See Figure 2.4**

Step 2: Now close your eyes and visualize these balloons in your mind. Try to classify your thoughts and emotions and

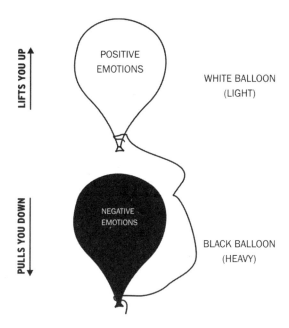

Our positive emotions set us free and lift us up whenever
our negative emotions bind us and pull us down.

FIGURE 2.4

place them in these two balloons—the positive thoughts in
the white balloon and the negative thoughts in the black
balloon. Imagine that the black balloon is slowly being
squeezed and losing its capacity to hold the white balloon
down, while the white balloon is becoming stronger and
stronger and is gradually rising from the surface, taking the
black one (which now has little air in it) along with it.

Step 3: As the white balloon increases in size and rises, the
black balloon loses all air and eventually disappears. Now,

with strong determination, cut off and throw away this useless black balloon. As this happens, the white balloon with all your positive emotions takes you to a higher plane and leaves the black balloon on the ground. Now you can go up and up without any restriction since you have cut off the negative thoughts and words from your mind. By repeating positive words, we put more air into our white balloon and, in a way, rise higher and higher.

Make a conscious effort to repeat this exercise, with your eyes closed, three to four times a day for the first week and then twice a day for the next six to eight weeks. You will gradually feel motivated to take action.

4. THE POWERFUL SYMBOL OF WORDS

Nightingale: The singing bird which soothes our heart through her melodious whistles is chosen as the symbol of the Power of Words. The magic of her songs forces people to pay

The symbol of the Power of Words

Nightingale

FIGURE 2.5

attention to her. The melody of her notes captivates listeners. Similar is the Power of Words. We should therefore learn from the nightingale to always say sweet and pleasing words to others. **See Figure 2.5**

5. AN EMPOWERING PERSONALITY

How the Power of Words helped Barack Obama become the first African-American president of the United States of America

His is an American story: values from the heartland, a middle-class upbringing in a strong family, hard work and education as the means of getting ahead, and the conviction that life should be lived in the service of others. US President Barack Obama was born in Hawaii on 4 August 1961. He was raised with help from his grandfather, who served in Patton's army, and his grandmother, who worked her way up from the secretarial pool to middle management at a bank.

He was elected the 44th president of the United States on 4 November 2008 and sworn in on 20 January 2009. During his presidential campaign, Obama came up with the slogan *'Change We Need'*. These powerful words struck a chord with the American people. And they went out, voted for him and made him the first African-American to reach the White House.

Obama has the rare ability to persuade a large number of people to his views. 'Obama's speeches . . . are almost plain, simple and to the point,' says Geoffrey Nunberg, a linguist. Obama's success can be credited to the characteristics common among great speakers. He speaks with confidence and conviction, yet is slightly distanced from his own words, showing conservatism, and a sense of control over his emotions. Obama is a great orator and speaks from a position of love, strength, conviction and principle, not from a position of hatred, weakness, doubt and deception.

Three important lessons can be learnt from Obama's life:

a) Positive words convey your intentions and help you to associate with people.

b) Your words shape your attitude and hence your destiny. You must be careful in selecting them.

c) Your positive words are an inspiration to others and help in changing your inner as well as outer world.

6. EIGHT EMPOWERING QUESTIONS

i. Am I thinking positive words when I am alone? Is my intention good when I think or say something?

ii. What new and positive words have I added to my vocabulary today? Am I practising them?

iii. Do my words inspire people whom I meet daily?

iv. Have I listened to the other person before speaking?

v. Do I pause and think before speaking?

vi. How can I be more effective in my communication? What more can I do to improve it?

vii. What am I doing to take charge of my negative emotions and stay positive today?

viii. When others are trying to get into an argument, am I able to avoid it?

7. EIGHT EMPOWERING AFFIRMATIONS

i. I live each day by choosing positive words that help me to excel.

ii. I learn empowering affirmations and repeat them to myself every day.

iii. I try to bring out the best in every person I meet through genuine appreciation.

iv. I consciously choose positive words while speaking and speak kindly to all.

v. I listen attentively to others to clearly understand what they mean to say.

vi. I enjoy each day and feel powerful, happy and excited as I engage in positive self-talk.

vii. I look for opportunities to communicate effectively. I avoid arguments.

viii. I enjoy life's challenges and always try to keep my word.

8. EIGHT TIPS TO HELP YOU ENHANCE YOUR POWER OF WORDS

1) **Choose your words carefully.** Words can have a positive or a negative impact in your life and that of others. Everything depends on the intention and emotions with which they are said. Every word that you say is powerful and should therefore be carefully chosen. If you are angry in a situation, count till ten before you say anything. This will save you from uttering damaging words.

2) **Guard your self-talk.** Your internal dialogue is the single most important factor that helps you achieve success.

Make sure you communicate with yourself positively at all times and keep adding new positive words to your vocabulary.

3) **Make a notebook of positive words and inspirational quotes.** Words, when used effectively, have the potential to inspire positive action. You should write down positive words and quotes in a notebook and dip into it a couple of times each day. Words can instil enthusiasm, create positive energy and bring out the best in us.

4) **Learn to say 'I'm sorry'.** You must learn to admit your mistakes as quickly as you become aware of them. This removes the feeling of guilt and prevents bad situations from worsening.

5) **Practise saying, and accepting, 'I forgive you.'** We all make mistakes. You must also accept that people around you will slip up. By making or accepting a sincere apology you save yourself and others from blame games, anxiety and guilt.

6) **Make a gratitude list.** Make a list of all the good things that have happened in your life and also a list of life's gifts to you. Update it from time to time. This will help you remember the people and things you should be grateful for. It will also lift your spirits.

7) **Learn positive communication to bring about positive results.** Positive communication with others will put your career on the fast track. If you stay positive and calm when others are losing their head, you become the master of the situation and are able to think clearly, while giving sufficient time to deciding about reacting or not.

8) **Keep your word and words will keep you in good stead.**
Always try to stick to your words and commitments. It
is an essential quality in a person of good character.
When you keep your commitments, people respect you
and look upon you as a responsible person. If it is not
possible for you to do something, saying a polite 'no' is
better than offering hope that you might be able to
perform the task later.

Success Principle #2:
Use the Power of Words

Think, speak, read, write and listen to only positive,
beautiful and affirmative words (as far as possible).
The words that touch you in any form affect you
strongly and shape your thoughts, attitudes and
character—the three foundations of success.

Three
The Power of Self-Confidence

1. Understanding the Power of Self-Confidence
2. How to develop your Power of Self-Confidence
3. An empowering exercise to unleash the Power of Self-Confidence within you
4. The powerful symbol of self-confidence
5. An empowering personality
6. Eight empowering questions
7. Eight empowering affirmations
8. Eight tips to help you enhance your self-confidence

1. UNDERSTANDING THE POWER OF SELF-CONFIDENCE

A businessman was deep in debt and could see no way out. Creditors were closing in on him. Suppliers were demanding payment. He sat on the park bench, head in hands, wondering if there was anything that could save his company from bankruptcy. Just at that moment an old man appeared before him.

'I can see that something is troubling you,' he said. After listening to the businessman's woes, the old man said, 'I believe I can help you.' He asked the man his name, wrote out a cheque and pushed it into his hands. 'Take this money,' he said. 'Meet me here exactly one year from today, and you can pay me back at that time.' Then the old man went away.

The businessman saw that he held a cheque for $500,000 signed by John D. Rockefeller, then one of the richest men in the world. 'I can erase my money worries in an instant,' he thought. But then he decided to put the uncashed cheque in his safe. Just knowing it was there might give him strength to work out a way to save his business, he thought.

With renewed optimism, he negotiated better deals and extended terms of payment. He closed several big sales. Within a few months, he was out of debt and making money again. Exactly a year later, he returned to the park with the uncashed cheque. At the agreed-upon time, the old man appeared.

But just as the businessman was about to hand back the cheque and share his success story, a nurse came running and grabbed the old man. 'I'm so glad I caught him,' she said. 'I hope he hasn't been bothering you. He's always escaping from the rest home and telling people he's John D. Rockefeller.' And she led the old man away by the arm.

The businessman just stood there, stunned. All year long he had been buying and selling and closing deals, convinced he had half a million dollars behind him. He now realized that it wasn't the money, real or imagined, that had turned his life around. It was his newfound self-confidence that gave him the power to achieve what he wanted.

This story shows that faith can move mountains. You now have a clear vision through the Power of Imagination. Soon you will learn how to pay attention to this vision through the

Power of Focus and how to set clear goals with the help of the Power of Goal Setting detailed later in the book.

But before you move ahead and enter the realm of action, you need the Power of Self-Confidence—without which your picture of the future may disappear into thin air. You need to unleash the Power of Self-Confidence from within you.

What is self-confidence?

Self-confidence is an attitude which helps to build a positive and realistic perception of ourselves and our abilities. It is about expressing our assertiveness, optimism, enthusiasm, affection, pride, independence and trust. Though we may be inspired in a moment to achieve something great in life, self-confidence is not built overnight. It is the affirmation and re-affirmation of positive and self-empowering beliefs. Our self-confidence is shaped by what we repeatedly tell our subconscious mind.

Self-confidence: the common denominator of success

The Power of Self-Confidence is one of the most important elements in the fulfillment of your dreams. It is a living force that puts an end to your inner conflicts and sceptical nature, and gives you the necessary momentum to achieve your goals. The Power of Self-Confidence causes amazing transformations. Confident people step up to become scientists, engineers, entrepreneurs, writers, artists, etc. These people prefer to control their environment and destiny. **See Figure 3.1**

One study of 500 successful people revealed a common factor. Every single person out of these 500 absolutely believed

Self-confidence

Affirmations

Positive thoughts   +   Self-empowering beliefs

THE POWER OF SELF-CONFIDENCE

FIGURE 3.1

that they were going to be a big success. They all faced setbacks, they all had their worries and ups and down, but they never lost sight of their vision to become successful. To be successful, you have to absolutely believe in yourself and your ability.

With self-confidence, you can achieve great things in life. The voice within, when trained to repeat only positive instructions, will strengthen your self-confidence. When all positive thoughts are put together, they form a positive belief system inside you. As you constantly reinforce your positive thoughts and reject all negative thoughts, you develop an enhanced level of self-confidence. The Power of Self-

Confidence awakens and encourages you to take a giant leap towards your goals. It is then that your heart, even before you take the first step, tells you that you are going to be successful.

> *'When it is dark enough, you can see the stars.'*
> —*Charles A. Beard*

After World War II, a small group of people gathered with its leaders in a burnt-out departmental store in devastated Tokyo. They had nothing but the strong belief that they could develop technologies that would help rebuild Japan's economy, which had been destroyed by the war. Those twenty people had the conviction that even though Japan did not have sufficient natural resources, it did have the necessary people-power.

The company they founded amid the debris was Sony, an immense success story today. What kept Akio Morita, the CEO of Sony Corporation, going was the Power of Self-Confidence.

> *'The future belongs to those who believe in the beauty of their dreams.'*
> —Eleanor Roosevelt

With self-confidence you can overcome all obstacles

There are many instances of people left with little or nothing finally prevailing on the strength of their self-confidence. Often the obstacles encountered on the way to achieving your objectives will seem too daunting. You may even start thinking of giving up. But don't. Have the courage to persist, hold on to your dreams and be willing to take one step ahead at a time. The Power of Self-Confidence has helped millions reach their goals; it can also help you achieve miracles.

The person who is certain to advance is the one who is too big for his place, who has a clear concept of what he wants to be, who knows that he can become what he wants to be, and who is determined to be what he wants to be.'

—*Anonymous*

Law of self-confidence

The law of self-confidence says that whatever you believe with certainty will become your reality. If you repeat something over and over to yourself, your subconscious mind starts believing it to be real. It cannot distinguish between positive and negative things. If you say to yourself 'I can't', it will believe it; if you say 'Yes, I can', it will believe that too. This is why affirmations are important: they act as self-motivators and help build confidence.

The Victor
'If you think you are beaten, you are.
If you think you dare not, you don't
If you like to win but think you can't,
It's almost a cinch you won't.

If you think you'll lose, you're lost.
For out in the world we find
Success begins with a fellow's will
It's all in the state of mind.

If you think you are outclassed, you are.
You've got to think high to rise.
You've got to be sure of yourself before
You can ever win the prize.

Life's battles don't always go
To the stronger or faster man.
But sooner or later, the man who wins
Is the man who thinks he can.'
—C.W. Longenecker

Self-confidence may have different meanings at different stages

For some people, self-confidence may be speaking in public; for others, it may be being confident in social situations or being self-assured. But self-confidence is more than just being 'not anxious or nervous'. It is a mix of the display of personal power, healthy self-esteem and regarding yourself as the equal of others.

Self-confidence acts as a lighthouse that constantly points you in the right direction. It is your belief in yourself and your goals. The growth of self-confidence starts from childhood. The belief system of a child who is repeatedly told that he is born to be great and successful and can achieve all that he wants, will be different from that of a child who is made to believe he cannot succeed no matter how hard he might try. But you can change your belief system over time by using some techniques explored later in this chapter.

'In the province of the mind, what one believes to be true either is true or becomes true.'
—John Lilly

Doubt and inferiority complex are common among beginners

All great achievers, all self-made millionaires and anyone who ever achieved anything worthwhile started with self-doubt. Most of us begin with doubt and an inferiority complex. Every man or woman who has ever achieved anything worthwhile went through a phase where they had little or no confidence. But they did not give up. With courage and faith in themselves, they one day set out on the long journey towards their goal. I am reminded of the great poem 'Don't Quit'.

Don't Quit

When things go wrong, as they sometimes will,
When the road you're trudging seems all uphill,
When the funds are low and the debts are high,
And you want to smile, but you have to sigh,
When care is pressing you down a bit,
Rest, if you must, but don't you quit.

Life is queer with its twists and turns,
As every one of us sometimes learns,
And many a failure turns about,
When he might have won had he stuck it out;
Don't give up though the pace seems slow—
You may succeed with another blow.

Often the goal is nearer than,
It seems to a faint and faltering man,
Often the struggler has given up,
When he might have captured the victor's cup,
And he learned too late when the night slipped down,
How close he was to the golden crown.

Success is failure turned inside out—
The silver tint of the clouds of doubt,
And you never can tell how close you are,
It may be near when it seems so far,
So stick to the fight when you're hardest hit—
It's when things seem worst that you must not quit.

—Anonymous

2. HOW TO DEVELOP YOUR POWER OF SELF-CONFIDENCE

Self-limiting beliefs are among the biggest obstacles to building self-confidence. You must try to get rid of the false notions you have been holding about yourself in your brain. To do this, you must write down the different beliefs that affect your performance and ask yourself: 'Is this attitude justified? Is it true about myself? What can I do to change it?'

When you analyze your self-limiting beliefs and ask self-empowering questions of yourself, you will find that most of your beliefs are false. Knowing this, you can adopt a new belief system that is self-empowering and enriching. **See Figure 3.2**

When you do this, you will realize that all your beliefs are a choice and what stands between you and your accomplishments is the will to take the first step and the belief that it is possible for you to reach the great heights of achievement.

Tips to enhance your self-confidence

Develop your self-esteem

Self-esteem is the opinion you have about yourself. It greatly influences you each time you go out to perform. The higher

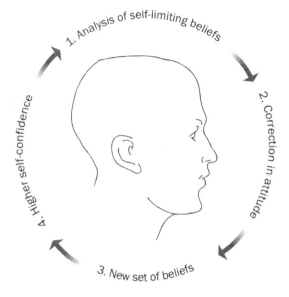

1. Analysis of self-limiting beliefs
2. Correction in attitude
3. New set of beliefs
4. Higher self-confidence

FIGURE 3.2

your self-esteem, the better your performance at work. Self-esteem and self-confidence have a direct correlation. One of the first steps to take when you want to build self-confidence is to like yourself. When you develop admiration for yourself, your self-respect and confidence level go up. Start saying to yourself from today, 'I like myself, I like myself, I like myself.'

Your self-esteem plays a major role even in your interactions with others. While dealing with other people, constantly remind yourself, 'I am as important as you are and you are as important as I am.' When you repeat this affirmation, your self-esteem and self-confidence are enhanced. When this happens, your chances of success in relationships increase. There is a direct correlation between the amount of self-respect you have and the respect others have for you.

'We often overestimate others and underestimate ourselves.'

—Shishir Srivastava

How to gain instant self-confidence

Getting over difficult situations is not always easy. Our brain tends to lock in memories when an event causes negative emotions. These strong emotions return when things go badly. Surely you remember forgetting a line in a poem when you were young or being pointed at when you didn't complete your homework. But you had a lot of successes too—and they were just as important.

The problem is that focusing on failures tends to lower self-confidence and lets you down. So you must recall your triumphs. Maintain a victory log. Instead of recalling your failures, summon up the instances where you did well. Each day write down one or two successes that you have had. Regularly feed your victory log and refer to it when you feel low. A look at it will boost your self-confidence.

Develop self-confidence through rehearsal

Be it an interview, an examination, an instance of public speaking or anything else, you can 'feel' the situation you are about to face—and, more important, prepare yourself for it—beforehand. The more you put yourself in real-life situations, the more your confidence will grow and the better your performance will be. So practise, practise, practise and your self-confidence will get a boost.

Focus on your strengths

You are born to excel in something. The best way to identify your ability is to put yourself in different situations. Then see what you like doing the most, what you can do with natural ease. Once you discover your innate talent, you must devote a great amount of time to working hard and trying to become the best in your chosen field. This will increase your confidence tremendously.

Learn to overcome your fears

Have the firm belief that you have the ability and strength to overcome your fears. Remember, fear is a state of mind. You may fear doing something but many others around you do the same thing with natural ease. Some of them would have started out with fear in their mind, just like you. These people should be an inspiration to you. To overcome your fears, you must choose to take small but consistent steps in the direction of what you fear doing.

When you do a bit of what you fear, your confidence gets a boost. Suppose you have never been on stage and have a fear of speaking in public. You can begin by learning a few lines from a poem that you like. Practise speaking the lines aloud in a room in front of a mirror and later on an empty stage (with no audience at all). This step-by-step process will bolster your faith in yourself. Slowly, you will reach a stage where you will be speaking in front of an audience with little or no fear at all.

Face criticism and gain emotional maturity

As you begin to raise your standards, you will often face criticism from co-workers and even from those you do not know. At such a time, remind yourself that what people think of you has no impact whatsoever on your career and that it cannot affect you until you yourself allow it to do so. What truly matters for your progress is the opinion you have about yourself. You must learn to handle criticism with grace and a smile, not with fear and frustration. Always think positively and remember that any criticism is better handled with a smile and emotional maturity than with a frown and a retort.

Learn to handle failure

There will be times when you will fail to achieve your goal. In such a situation you should recognize that failure is never final. You must use it to enrich your experience and learn from your mistakes. Have faith in the future and believe that everything will finally be all right. This belief will keep your spirits up and not let failure affect you.

Motivate yourself by doing small things

When you start taking smart steps consistently, your confidence level will go up. You will feel livelier, walk faster, talk louder and speak with more confidence. When such things happen, do remember to give yourself a pat on the back.

Do not compare yourself with others

You are a unique person. If you compare yourself with others, you actually show lack of respect for yourself. Instead, learn to compare yourself with yourself—that is, the kind of person you are now and the kind of person you wish to be.

To become the person you would like to be, you must compete with yourself. Each time you do something good, reward yourself. Thereafter, challenge yourself to improve your next performance and start preparing. Each time you focus on improving your performance—retaining the things you did right, rejecting those you did wrong—your self-confidence will grow.

'Your biggest competition is yourself.'
—Shishir Srivastava

3. AN EMPOWERING EXERCISE TO UNLEASH THE POWER OF SELF-CONFIDENCE WITHIN YOU

Find a quiet room in your house and place a mirror there. Stand in a relaxed position in front of the mirror and take half-a-dozen deep breaths. Now look straight into your eyes and see yourself. 'This' is you, your present self. Recall your deepest desire and close your eyes. Imagine that you have achieved your goal and how you will look after achieving it. You feel successful, confident and empowered. Keep your eyes closed and say to yourself, 'Yes, I can do it. Yes, I'm doing it.' Repeat these affirmations again and again till you are comfortable with them.

Gradually open your eyes and establish eye contact with your image in the mirror. Take a deep breath and hold it. With this breath, hold your image of the future and assure yourself that you are 'this'. Release your breath gently and feel relaxed.

Repeat this exercise twice a day, once after you get up in the morning and once before going to bed. Within a week you will feel a great surge in your confidence level.

'When you come to the edge of all the light you know and are about to step off into the darkness of the unknown, faith is knowing one of the two things will happen: there will be something solid to stand on or you will be taught to fly.'
—Barbara Winter

4. THE POWERFUL SYMBOL OF SELF-CONFIDENCE

Mountain: A mountain is the symbol of self-confidence because it stands firm and unshaken in all kinds of weather. It challenges us to climb and conquer it; it stands as a test of our self-confidence. When you look at a mountain with the thought of climbing it, it echoes, 'Climb up not just to measure my height, but your self-confidence too.' When one thinks of moving it, a mountain whispers, 'If you've the courage and the confidence, come on and move me. I know you can.' It is a symbol of hope and inspiration for all who think of climbing or moving it. **See Figure 3.3**

The symbol of the Power of Self-Confidence

Mountain

FIGURE 3.3

'One person with a belief is a social power equal to ninety-nine who have only interests.'
—John Stuart Mill

5. An Empowering Personality

How the Power of Self-Confidence helped A.R. Rahman become one of the best music composers in the world

Allah Rakha Rahman was born A.S. Dileep Kumar on 6 January 1966 in a family of musicians in Madras. He started learning the piano at the age of four. He was nine when his father died. Under pressure to support his family, he joined film composer Ilayaraja's troupe as a keyboard player at the age of eleven. Although he had to drop out of school because of this, he got to travel across the world with various orchestras.

During childhood, Rahman was a shy singer and only practised with the lights off. Gradually, he overcame his fears and developed enough confidence to first practise with the lights on and then to sing in front of people.

In 2008, Rahman's work gained global prominence when his score for *Slumdog Millionaire* won him two Academy Awards. Today, the 'Mozart of Madras' is widely accepted as the man who redefined contemporary Indian music.

Three important lessons can be learnt from Rahman's life:

a) The biggest hurdle between you and your goals are your fears. So you must face your fears with courage and learn to conquer them.

b) You are your best friend. So be confident and try to excel at whatever you are good at.

c) With the Power of Self-Confidence you can achieve great heights in life, no matter where you stand today.

6. Eight empowering questions

    i. Am I holding fast to old belief patterns?

    ii. What new beliefs have I adopted today?

    iii. Which new path is my self-confidence telling me to take?

    iv. How can I fulfil my potential?

    v. What am I doing to enhance my self-confidence?

    vi. What kind of risks am I willing to take?

    vii. What should I do when my self-confidence 'tells' me that I will succeed if I try?

    viii. Do I feel enthusiastic when I realize that my self-confidence is firm and I can achieve what I want to?

7. Eight empowering affirmations

    i. I am feeling an enhanced level of confidence.

    ii. I'm building upon my self-confidence today and feel myself changing and improving each day.

    iii. I dream and have confidence in my dreams. I believe I can fulfil my dreams.

    iv. My mind, body and soul are working in unity and helping me achieve my goals.

    v. As my mental blocks fade away, I realize there are infinite opportunities and possibilities around me. When I look at my work, I say to myself, 'Yes, I can do it.'

    vi. I am overcoming all obstacles with the Power of Self-Confidence in me.

    vii. I perform with the attitude of doing more than is required of me. I constantly innovate and upgrade my skills.

viii. The image of my goal is clear in my mind and I am taking steps to reach there.

8. EIGHT TIPS TO ENHANCE YOUR SELF-CONFIDENCE

1) **Self-confidence is formed through positive beliefs.** Self-confidence comes through repetitive affirmation. It is strengthened by positive thoughts that give us courage and confidence to do things right. As you start believing in yourself, your self-confidence builds up.

2) **Self-confidence encourages you to take a new direction.** When you find that something is not working in your life, your self-confidence will encourage you to take a new direction. However distant the fresh destination may look, the Power of Self-Confidence within will make you act and advance in this direction. Take the first step and start moving. While many such small steps will lead you towards your goal, others will see the process as one giant leap.

3) **Self-confidence acts as an accelerator.** Self-confidence acts as an accelerator, driving you towards your goals. It gives you the momentum needed to overcome all obstacles and hindrances. We have the ability to express the greatness that lies dormant within us. Only when you look inside and have confidence in your goals can you start expressing your creative energy.

4) **Self-confidence grows through cooperation.** To strengthen your self-confidence, you need to express your creativity through cooperation. Seek help from your own body, mind and soul so that they work in harmony with each other. Seek assistance from your family members, friends and acquaintances. As you help others attain their goals and get their cooperation in

accomplishing your own goals, your self-confidence will soar.

5) **Self-confidence draws your attention to possibilities.** As the Power of Self-Confidence is released from within, your mind opens up to new possibilities. You become aware of the opportunities surrounding you. This is because your self-confidence expands and the voice within tells you, 'Yes, it can be done.'

6) **Self-confidence can overcome all obstacles.** When you start working towards your goals, you might face huge challenges. But your self-confidence should stand higher than these hurdles. As you take on various tasks, one at a time, you will find them easy to do.

7) **You gain self-confidence by finishing small tasks.** Break your goal into doable parts and start taking action, one step at a time. Your confidence will increase with each step you take.

8) **You will recognize if you have confidence in yourself and your goal.** As your performance levels go up, so will your self-confidence. You will gradually understand that what you have imagined for yourself is within reach. An image of achieving the goal will start appearing in your mind. And if you believe in it, you will see it happen too.

Success Principle #3:
Use the Power of Self-Confidence

Have full confidence in your powers. Keep telling yourself that your future will evolve just the way you want it to—and that this will happen sooner rather than later.

Four
The Power of Goal Setting

1. UNDERSTANDING THE POWER OF GOAL SETTING

A Harvard case study

In 1979 a study was conducted at the Harvard Business School involving graduating students. They were asked if they had set clear written goals for the future and had plans to accomplish them. Only 3 per cent of the students had written goals and plans. Thirteen per cent had goals, but had not written them down. And 84 per cent had no specific goals at all, aside from getting out of school and enjoying the summer.

Ten years later, in 1989, the same students were interviewed again. The study found that the 13 per cent who had had goals but had not written them down were earning, on average, twice as much as the 84 per cent students who had had no goals at all. But more surprisingly, the 3 per cent who had had clear, written goals when they left Harvard were earning, on average, *ten times* as much as the other 97 per cent *put together*. The only difference between the three groups of students was the clarity of the goals they had set for themselves when they started out.

This case study establishes the importance of goal setting in our lives and how it greatly influences our performance.

What are goals?

Goals are written statements that provide a meaningful direction to your life. They help you concentrate your energy on the path of achievement and fulfilment. So it is essential that you define your heart's desire in specific terms: with a deadline and a written goal statement. This way you will give a clear direction to your life. Goals act like a compass on the ship of your life; without them you will keep floating midway, with nowhere special to go.

Someone has rightly said, 'Success is goals and all else is commentary.' You must learn how to set goals and achieve them. Once you have mastered the art of setting goals, you can apply it to any area of your life and double your productivity from the very first week.

> *'Goals provide us the energy source that powers our lives. One of the best ways we can get the most from the energy we have is to focus it. That is what goals can do for us: focus our energy.'*
>
> —Denis Waitley

How a goal differs from a dream

The difference between a dream and a goal is that a goal is clearly defined in writing and has a specific deadline. Dreams are merely wishes or fantasies. Goals help you to increase

FIGURE 4.1

your focus. They give you momentum by making you fully aware of the direction in which your work is taking you. Therefore, having a written goal statement is much better than having no goal at all. See **Figure 4.1**

> '*The difference between a goal and a dream is the written word.*'
>
> —Gene Donohue

Why set goals?

During my presentations, members of the audience often ask me, 'Why should I set goals? Can't I do without them?' I reply, 'You certainly can. Not everyone who has achieved great results learnt how to set goals first. But what they achieved in ten to twenty years, you can achieve in five years or less by the Power of Goal Setting.'

Our mind works best when it is up against challenges that have to be met within a reasonable time frame.

For example, if you want to double your income without setting a goal, then with 5 per cent to 10 per cent annual increment you will automatically double it in ten to twenty years. But that will be too long a wait, isn't it? Especially when it is possible to double your income in three years—by writing it down as a goal statement, taking concrete steps and reviewing your progress on a weekly and monthly basis.

> '*Goals are the fuel in the furnace of achievement.*'
>
> —Tom Hopkins

Goals and categories

One of the best things about goal statements is that you can use them in various aspects of your life. You can set goals regarding, say, personal matters, career advancement and social contribution. When people think of goals, they mostly think of career alone. But you can have other objectives in life too.

Why don't you set goals in a variety of areas so that you develop a complete personality? Here are a few ideas:

i) **Personal:** Education, family, friends, personal development (health, nutrition, fitness, skills, spirituality), home and travel

ii) **Career:** Career, business, finance, savings, income and investments

iii) **Contribution to society:** Volunteer work focusing on people, environment, etc.

2. HOW TO DEVELOP YOUR POWER OF GOAL SETTING

Here is an effective goal-setting and goal-achieving strategy. You may not get immediate results but the following technique will increase your focus and productivity from day one.

Writing a goal statement

Remember these essential five steps when writing a powerful goal statement:

Step 1: Find your peak energy time. Write the statement during your peak energy hour. It could be the morning or the afternoon. You may want to play your favourite music to lift your spirits.

Step 2: Start writing. Take a pen and a white sheet of paper. Write the date and a list of 10 things that you aspire for.

Step 3: Identify your most important goal. Out of these 10 goals on your list, encircle the one which, if achieved in the next year, will have the biggest positive impact in your life and career. Write down this goal on the other side of the paper too.

Step 4: Decide on a deadline. A goal can be best defined as 'a realistic dream with a specific deadline'. You must aim to achieve a goal within a time frame that forces you to act fast. To do this, you must ask yourself, 'What is the approximate time it will take me to accomplish my goal?' Then, whatever is that time, reduce it by half. If you think it will take you two years to get something, aim to achieve it in one year and write the deadline on top of your most important goal. This will keep reminding you of *where you are* vis-à-vis *where you have to go*.

Step 5: Write down your goal statement. It is important to keep three things in mind:

(i) **All goal statements start with 'I'.** Remember that the goal statement is yours. When you put 'I' at the very start, it becomes personalized.

(ii) **Write your goal statement in the present tense.** The 'I' should be followed by a verb expressed in the present tense. This is because the subconscious mind reads and believes only in the present. If you talk to your brain in the future tense and say 'I want to' or 'I wish to', it reads these as 'wanting' or 'wishing' thoughts. Result: your conscious brain cannot do anything about them. Your brain will see this work as something to be done in the future. To put real power behind your goals, you must write them down in the future tense.

(iii) **Express your goals with positive words.** Instead of saying 'I want to lose 10 kg in three months', say 'I will weigh XX kg three months from now.' Life mostly unfolds the way you expect it to. Stick to your goals with positive expectations and work with passion. This will quicken the process of goal achievement.

Your goal statements should be easy to understand. Even a child should be able to figure out what you are aiming for. Once you have written a clear statement regarding your most important goal, you can jot down statements about other areas of your life. Here are a few examples of goal statements:

i) I, Rita Sharma, am savouring the beautiful view from the window of my new home. Deadline: _____

ii) I, Ashish Mehra, am enjoying driving my brand-new BMW. Deadline: _____

iii) I, Priya Malhotra, am running a successful business. Deadline: _____

iv) I, Rahul Gupta, am feeling thrilled at graduating from the Harvard Business School. Deadline: _____

v) I, Sonia Nigam, love to exercise daily and am enjoying being at my ideal weight of 58 kg. I am fit and in excellent shape. Deadline: _____

Write in as much detail as possible

If you want a home, don't just write 'a beautiful new home'. Instead note down, 'A house set in five acres of land, with four bedrooms, a study and a view of the mountains.' The more information you give your subconscious mind, the better it will be able to work towards reaching the goal. To do this, you can use the Power of Imagination to visualize the kind of home you want. Imagine walking around the house. See yourself standing on the porch off the master bedroom, the mountains shrouded in mist and the kitchen garden full of tomatoes, green beans and cucumbers.

After writing your goal statement on paper, note it down on a pocket-sized index card. Keep this card for reference and read your goal statement often.

God at the counter

A woman dreamt that she walked into a shop and found God behind the counter.

'What do you sell here?' she asked.

'Everything your heart desires,' said God.

The woman decided to ask for the best things she could think of. 'I want peace of mind, love, happiness, wisdom and freedom from fear,' she said. As an afterthought she added, 'Not just for me. For everyone on Earth.'

God smiled. 'I think you've got me wrong, my dear,' He said. 'We don't sell fruits here. Only seeds.'

Develop a long-term perspective

'We often overestimate what we can achieve in a year and underestimate what we can achieve in ten years!'
—**Anthony Robbins**

In the process of goal setting, it is important to have a long-term perspective. You will plan and work better once you really know where you would like to see yourself in five to ten years.

Many people set big goals but give themselves only a year or so to meet them. This only leads to frustration and stress. Any major goal requires a substantial amount of time to be accomplished. A tree often needs three or more years to grow and bear fruit; it cannot do so in just one year. **See Figure 4.2**

Developing a Long-Term Perspective

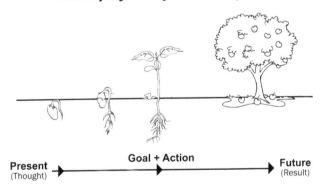

Present (Thought) → **Goal + Action** → **Future** (Result)

A goal is like a seed sown in the present. It first becomes a sapling, then a plant and eventually a fruit-bearing tree.

FIGURE 4.2

Make sure your goal is high enough

Someone rightly said, *'Aim to shoot for the highest stars, in case you miss them you will land on Mars!'* When you set your eyes on a big goal, you work hard and stretch your capabilities to achieve it. But if your goal is not challenging enough, you are unlikely to leave your comfort zone—and the result will be little or no success.

> *'You've got to do your own growing, no matter how tall your grandfather was.'*
>
> —**Irish proverb**

Three laws of developing the Power of Goal Setting

(a) **The Law of Correspondence:** Your outer world corresponds to your inner world of goal setting. That is, whatever you have within will reflect outside.

Application of the Law of Correspondence: By using this law the plans you have in mind can come to fruition.

(b) **The Law of Subconscious Activity:** Your subconscious mind alerts you to the things around you that are consistent with your dominant desires and concerns.

Application of the Law of Subconscious Activity: By using this law you can give your subconscious mind a clear picture of your goals. The subconscious will arrange all your words and actions so that they fit in a pattern consistent with achieving your aims.

(c) **The Law of Habit:** Virtually all that you do is automatic, the result of habit. Keep or develop the habits that take you towards your goals; give up those that take you away from what you want to attain.

Application of the Law of Habit: By using this law you can develop the good habits that will help make your desires come true.

Applying these three laws in your life along with the Power of Goal Setting will boost your chances of success.

Resolve today to become a peak performer

Any crucial change in your life takes place when you decide to do a thing, decide to stop doing it or decide not to do anything at all. You can only become efficient when you start taking clear decisions in key areas of your life. Master the art of doing essential things first, whether you like doing them or not.

Practise daily planning and goal setting

Follow the '6P' formula: Prior Proper Planning Prevents Poor Performance. Write down a detailed plan. Make a master list of everything you need to do to accomplish your goals. At the beginning of each month, draw up a list of tasks that have to be done. You can prepare such a list for each week and day too. This will help in keeping count of the amount of work you are getting done.

Become absolutely clear

Assign a deadline for each task that needs to be done and write it down. If you are clear about what you want, your chances of succeeding go up by 50 per cent.

Make a list of all that you need to do, prepare a plan around this list, organize yourself according to this plan and work to fulfil your goals. Determine how much money you want to earn, how much you want to weigh, how much time you want to spend with your family. Put down your goals in writing, read them often, set a deadline and force yourself to work hard every single day.

Use the 'A, B, C, D, E' formula

Make a list and prioritize your tasks:

A: Something very important

B: Something you should be doing

C: Something nice to do but that does not take you closer to your goal

D: Something you can delegate and outsource

E: Something that is not required to be done at all. (These are the tasks you should eliminate from your list.)

You can prioritize further—subdividing, say, the entry A into A1, A2, A3 and so on. Do this every day so that this formula becomes second nature. The idea is that you shouldn't do a 'B' item if an 'A' item is still pending. You shouldn't attempt an 'A3' item if 'A1' and 'A2' items are unfinished.

Apply the Pareto Principle

The Pareto Principle is based on the 80/20 rule that says 20 per cent of the things you do will account for the value of the other 80 per cent activities on your list. The reverse of this principle would be that 80 per cent of what you do will account for 20 per cent of what you will get. So practise creative procrastination: defer the 80 per cent of the low-value jobs and stick to the 20 per cent of the highest-value jobs. Do your biggest, ugliest and most challenging task FIRST! Don't just look at it or procrastinate. Start working

Out of ten tasks, the two most important ones will produce greater results than the other eight combined.

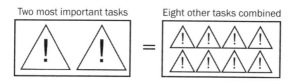

FIGURE 4.3

on it immediately and seek to finish it. This way you will become more productive. **See Figure 4.3**

3. AN EMPOWERING EXERCISE TO UNLEASH THE POWER OF GOAL SETTING WITHIN YOU

Take a blank sheet of paper and a pen. Think of the one goal that you have been trying to achieve for the past many days but have not been able to focus on. Now try this:

Step 1: Write down this goal on a piece of paper and look at it. Focus your attention on it for 20 seconds. Stop doing everything else and just focus on this one goal.

Step 2: Think of the first step you should take to achieve this goal. Do not think of the second step. Focus your attention on the first step you will take and write it down. Take some action related to this step: making a phone call, getting up and looking for a book or whatever. Take that action, now.

Step 3: You will see that as soon you take one step, the next will come into view, then the next and so on. So you need not worry about all the steps at the start. Just work on one step at a time and the next step will become clear.

'You don't have to see the entire staircase. Take the first step in faith and the next one will appear.'
—Martin Luther King Jr

4. THE POWERFUL SYMBOL OF GOAL SETTING

Fire: The energy that engulfs the strongest metals is chosen as the symbol of the Power of Goal Setting. Fire symbolizes warmth, hope and the capacity to engulf everything that comes in its way. Similarly, the Power of Goal Setting erases all the 'things to do'—through completion. **See Figure 4.4**

The symbol of the Power of Goal Setting

Fire

FIGURE 4.4

5. AN EMPOWERING PERSONALITY

How the Power of Goal Setting helps E. Sreedharan reach all his targets on time

Elattuvalapil Sreedharan, born on 11 July 1932, is a technocrat best known for his work on the Konkan Railway and Delhi Metro projects.

In 1963, a huge tidal wave washed away parts of the Pamban Bridge that connected Rameshwaram to mainland Tamil Nadu. The railways set a target of six months for the bridge to be repaired. Sreedharan's boss, under whose jurisdiction the bridge came, said the work had to be finished in three months. Sreedharan, who was put in charge, got the bridge repaired in just 46 days.

In 1990, after retirement, Sreedharan was entrusted with the 760-km Konkan Railway project. The assignment included constructing over 150 bridges and digging 93 tunnels stretching to 82 km. Under Sreedharan's stewardship, the task was completed in seven years. That a public-sector project could be completed without significant cost and time overruns was considered an achievement by many.

He was later made managing director of the Delhi Metro Rail Corporation. By mid-2005, all the scheduled sections of the rapid transit system had been completed on or before time and within their respective budgets. More Metro lines are under construction today.

Sreedharan meets his goals by dividing the project between sub-managers and giving them a deadline. He reviews daily progress reports and meets top staff and consultants each week. Sreedharan wakes up before dawn.

He meditates and does yoga in the morning and walks for 45 minutes in the evening.

Three important lessons that can be learnt from Sreedharan's life:

a) You should set definite and time-bound goals to measure your progress.

b) You should review your goals from time to time.

c) You should constantly challenge and motivate yourself and your team to achieve your goals ahead of time.

6. EIGHT EMPOWERING QUESTIONS

i. Have I read my goals today?

ii. Have I made a plan to achieve them?

iii. What am I doing to achieve my goals?

iv. When was the last time I achieved success?

v. How can I repeat that success?

vi. Am I reminding myself about my goals?

vii. Is my determination sufficient to reach my goals?

viii. What will I look like when I have reached my goals?

7. EIGHT EMPOWERING AFFIRMATIONS

i. I set my daily goals based on my strongest desire.

ii. I read my goals daily and think of them often.

iii. I take action on my daily goals.

iv. I review my goals weekly to check my progress.

v. Every daily goal that I achieve makes me happy.

vi. I see infinite possibilities before me.

vii. I see myself achieving all my goals one by one and feel confident.

viii. As I achieve my goals in life, I help others to achieve theirs.

8. EIGHT TIPS TO DEVELOP YOUR POWER OF GOAL SETTING

We need constant reminders to focus on what we want. To focus better and achieve your goals, you must do the following:

1) **Divide your goals into workable parts.** Just as you cannot eat all the food served on a platter in a single step but have to eat it bite by bite, your goals have to be divided into small manageable parts and then worked upon. You can divide your major goals into sub-goals and set sub-deadlines.

2) **Read your goal statements often.** Try to read your goal statements at least twice a day. Initially read them just before sleeping and then immediately after getting up. The subconscious brain continues to function even after you fall asleep. It can register your goals and work on them throughout the night. When you get up, you will be more driven to work.

3) **Believe in your goals.** When you put faith in your aims, you add more power behind them. This improves your chances of achieving what you want.

4) **Take action daily.** To accomplish your goals on time, work on them every day. Sometimes you may not be able to give your best to your work. Still, do what little you can. This way you will move at least one step closer to your goal.

5) **Measure your goals.** Goal achievement also requires an effective feedback mechanism. Your brain should know how much you have achieved and how much remains to be accomplished, and you must work accordingly. A daily, weekly and monthly goal analysis will reveal how much you have achieved.

6) **Be flexible.** The goal statements written in the present tense serve as your 'immediate guiding system' and the deadline as a 'forcing system'. You then act as a heat-seeking missile locked to the target. When the target changes its position, you should be ready to change accordingly and chase it till you shoot it down. Remain flexible with the moving target. The most important rule of flexibility: be clear about your goal but be flexible about the process of achieving it.

7) **Start at the beginning.** Before you set off towards fulfilling your goals, determine your exact situation today. Be honest and realistic about what you want to accomplish in the future.

8) **Measure your progress.** Set clear benchmarks for yourself and keep assessing your progress. This will show how well you are doing and enable you to make necessary adjustments and corrections along the way.

'Twenty years from now you will be more disappointed by the things that you didn't do than by the ones you

did do. So throw off the bowlines. Sail away from the safe harbour. Catch the trade winds in your sails. Explore. Dream. Discover.'

—Mark Twain

Success Principle #4:
Use the Power of Goal Setting

Set your goals in the direction of what you want and love to do the most. Keep the burning desire alive in your heart and act with a calm mind.

Five
The Power of Focus

1. UNDERSTANDING THE POWER OF FOCUS

There was a time when I was required to handle many things. I was confused. I decided to act on one task at a time. I printed a black dot on a piece of paper, wrote 'Focus Now' below it and pasted the paper in front of my desk. During the day I would often focus my attention on the dot and read the instruction below it. **See Figure 5.1**

While working, I used to say 'focus now' to myself many times. This simple exercise increased my concentration

76

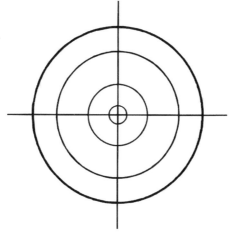

Focus Now!

THE POWER OF FOCUS

FIGURE 5.1

manifold and I discovered the Power of Focus within me. You too have this power.

What is Focus?

'Concentrate all your thoughts upon the work at hand. The sun's rays do not burn until brought to a focus.'
—Alexander Graham Bell

We discussed the Power of Imagination earlier. That power helps you visualize and create clear mental images about what you want to achieve in life. You need the Power of Focus to bring these mental images to reality. Focusing prevents your thoughts from wandering. The result: you are able to give full attention to important work.

The Power of Focus kicks into action when you want one thing more strongly than others. These thoughts are shaped into words and these words are transformed into action with the combined effort of your body, mind and soul. That you are reading this book and have reached this far shows that deep within you is a fire whose brightness will show you the way ahead. Your desire fuels this fire.

When you focus on a particular thing long and hard enough, your performance improves. You will receive greater rewards in life if you give proper attention to your goals.

Importance of focus

When C.V. Raman was young, he once tried to light a matchstick by making the sun's rays converge with the help of a hand lens. Since his hand was fidgety, the experiment failed. Then Raman's father came to his aid. He held Raman's hand tightly and asked him to slow down his breath and focus all his attention on the point where the matchstick was supposed to start burning. Raman did so and within seconds he accomplished what he had been trying to do for an hour. The incident taught him a big lesson. He decided to focus his entire attention on the work in hand. He went on to become a successful scientist and in 1930 won the Nobel Prize in Physics for discovering the Raman effect.

Just like the hand lens which Raman used, our mind has the great ability to make all our energy converge on a single point. When you concentrate on the present, your chances of finding the right solutions and taking the right steps increase dramatically. **See Figure 5.2**

Focus on the work in hand

FIGURE 5.2

Focus on the things you want

Someone has rightly said, 'If you always do what you have always done, you will always get what you have always got.' Your life starts to improve the day you stop doing the things you do not want to do and shift your focus to thinking about and doing the things you really want to do.

You should do the things you want to do and not the ones other people wish you to do. Take any one goal that you desperately want to achieve and for the next 24 hours think about it as much as you can. You can write about this goal and imagine achieving it. Even this simple step will heighten your excitement and enthusiasm. Now you can make a detailed plan to achieve the goal. Start acting on this plan from the next day and you will discover that your life will never be the same again.

Your mind's special ability

The brain has an organ called the reticular cortex that has the ability to recognize objects of desire and things associated with those objects. It is thus designed to help you recognize things, opportunities and people corresponding to what you are looking for. So once you focus your attention, you start to move rapidly towards your goals.

To understand this ability, let us do a quick exercise. Look around and count all the things that are red in colour. Now stop, close your eyes and try to recall the things that were white in colour. Do you remember? Certainly not. Now look around again. You will find that there are many white things that you failed to notice because you were only looking for red-coloured objects. This shows that we only find what we seek. It is rightly said, 'Seek and you shall find.'

Let us take another example. If you go to the airport to receive someone, you will notice your guest's flight number and its status again and again; the details of other flights will hold no value for you. But at that very moment another person might only be noticing the status of a different flight altogether. Thus we will have two people looking at the same display board but with a different focus. This shows that we tend to closely associate with things that matter the most to us.

Your Power of Focus can help you recognize meaningful information and opportunities with ease, provided you know what you want and concentrate on getting that.

Focus on positive things

You get what you focus on. So resolve to focus on doing things that will make a positive difference to your life and stay away from things that will have little or no impact.

For example, if you are overweight, stop saying 'I don't want to be fat and overweight.' Rather, focus on what you really want: 'a fit body', 'to be an active and agile person' or 'to have a balanced diet and healthy living'. You can attain positive things only by focusing on them.

Find time to do the things you want to do

You might complain you don't get enough time during the day to do the things you really want to do. That is understandable. Here you need to change your self-talk from 'I don't have time' or 'I'm too busy' to 'How can I find time?' or 'When can I do it? When you start thinking differently, you will begin to find the time.

To increase your focus, make a list of activities you need to do during the next 24 hours. Then concentrate on doing the most important things first and start doing them. It is rightly said that 'It is the act of taking the first step that separates winners from losers.' Take that first step, now.

Work of the spirits

A woodcarver called Ching had just finished work on a bell frame. Everyone marvelled at his creation because it seemed to be the work of spirits. When the Duke of Lu saw it, he asked, 'What sort of genius is yours that you could make such a thing?'

The woodcarver replied, 'Sir, I am only a simple workman. I am no genius. But there is one thing. When I am going to make a bell frame, I meditate for three days to calm my mind. When I have meditated for three days, I think no more about rewards or emoluments. When I have meditated for five days, I no longer think of praise or blame. When I have meditated for seven days, I forget my limbs, my body; no, I forget my very self, I lose consciousness of my surroundings. Only my skill remains.

'In that state I walk into the forest and examine each tree until I find one in which I see the bell frame in all its perfection. Then my hands go to the task. Having set myself aside, nature meets nature in the work that is performed through me. This, no doubt, is the reason why everyone says that the finished product is the work of the spirits.'

—Excerpt from *Taking Flight*

2. HOW TO DEVELOP YOUR POWER OF FOCUS

You have now understood what the Power of Focus is and the various aspects associated with it. Here is how you can develop and enrich your life with this power. **See Figure 5.3.**

Define your purpose

It is essential at this moment that you define your purpose. As Zig Ziglar says, *'Instead of becoming a wandering generality, you must become a meaningful specific.'* All successful people have a clearly defined purpose and at the outset of every endeavour they look towards its end. You must define what you want in each area of your life: health, career, family, travel and finances. Sit down and write what exactly you want and then spell out the price you are ready

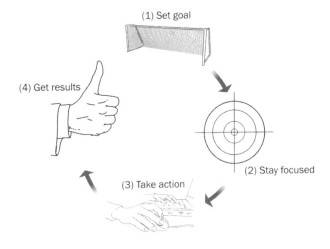

FIGURE 5.3

to pay along the journey. Once you are clear about these two important aspects, you will become a focused person.

> *'You can have anything you want—if you want it badly enough. You can be anything you want to be, do anything you set out to accomplish if you hold to that desire with singleness of purpose.'*
>
> —Abraham Lincoln

Six levels of focus based on time frame

Define specifically what you want in the following five time frames and ask yourself these important questions:

i. **Lifetime**—What do you want to become in life?

ii. **Yearly**—Keeping your life's purpose in mind, what one thing would you like to achieve in the next one year?

iii. **Monthly**—Keeping your yearly goal in mind, what are your targets this month?

iv. **Weekly**—What is your biggest challenge this week—keeping this month's target in mind?

v. **Daily**—Over the next 24 hours, what is the most important task you need to do to fulfil your weekly target?

vi. **Current**—What should you be doing at this moment to achieve your target for the day? Are you doing it?

Constantly ask yourself these questions. And remember that all levels of focus are equally important.

The artist Picasso attributed his success more to focus than creativity. He said that when he was creating art, he completely forgot himself and gave himself over to the job in hand. He thus became one with his work.

How to control your thoughts

Your mind is constantly thinking about one thing or the other. If you are thinking without a purpose, your thoughts will wander in all directions. To achieve something worthwhile, you need to focus your thoughts for a long duration.

To do this, you need to disassociate yourself from your thoughts for some time and 'come out of your mind' to become a 'thought observer'. You will notice that though you cannot stop thinking completely, you can check and mould the direction of your thoughts—just as the flow of a river cannot be stopped but can be diverted. So if you are thinking in a negative direction, you can divert your thoughts towards your purpose in a positive way. This is possible when you are clear about what you want and focus your mind on getting it. You must ask, 'What am I thinking? Is it worthy of my time? Is it related to the job in hand?' If not, you must immediately say no to all such thoughts and focus your entire attention on the present moment.

Zoom in, zoom out

In 2007 I was invited to the award presentation ceremony of the World's Children's Prize for the Rights of the Child in Sweden. There I met Magnus Bergmar, the CEO of the World's Children's Prize Foundation, a Sweden-based NGO that runs the world's largest children's education programme on democracy. In less than a decade, this programme has reached 102 countries involving 23 million students in 55,000 schools and organizations, including millions of vulnerable children, former child soldiers, refugees and children in conflict zones.

When I asked Bergmar how he organized such a mammoth project, he told me about the 'zoom in, zoom out' technique he used. Bergmar explained that when he wanted to focus on a particular task he would 'zoom in' and say no to everything else, thus giving his 100 per cent to the job in hand. Once the work was over, Bergmar would zoom out of that particular task. I found this approach very helpful when I applied it in my work and writing, and my focus increased tremendously. **See Figure 5.4**

Control your breath

Fragmented attention implies fragmented body movements. To achieve a goal, rapt attention is essential, accompanied by a still body with little or no movement. Find a comfortable place and stop fidgeting. Close your eyes, slow down your breath and subdue your negative impulses. Positive and

Zoom in

Zoom out

FIGURE 5.4

valuable thoughts direct you in the direction of your goals; all other thoughts must take a back seat. Slowly the mind will be trained to gain control over your emotions.

Each time your mind wanders, bring it to the present moment. Consciously remove all unwanted thoughts and eventually you will be able to wipe out all extraneous thoughts. Try to make your surroundings free from distractions, so you can concentrate well and for a longer duration.

Shifting targets now and then will lead your nowhere. You must decide in specific terms what you want to achieve and go after it single-mindedly. You must learn to control your mind and use it to achieve your purpose. Therefore, you must choose certain targets to be met during the day and work with full commitment and concentration to meet them.

A.P.J. Abdul Kalam, the former president who is popularly known as the 'Missile Man of India', says there were times when he was so absorbed in his work that he felt a 'great flow' and completely forgot his hunger, fatigue and sometimes even himself!

Top performers often experience such a 'flow' during their peak working hours.

Avoid distractions

To become a peak performer using the Power of Focus, you must avoid all kinds of distractions. There are two kinds of distractions:

a) **Internal distractions**: These are caused by our own thoughts and emotions. For example, you will find it difficult to concentrate on your work if you are hungry or have just had a fight with a colleague. So, learn how to gain control over such distractions and do not let them affect you.

Exercise self-control and keep in mind that nothing (and no one) can make you unhappy without your consent.

b) **External distractions**: Disturbances such as noise, constant phone calls, talkative co-workers and interfering bosses can cause external distractions. But you must not allow yourself to get irritated or anxious—and if you do, you must not let that affect your performance.

Train yourself to get back to work each time a distraction pops up.

Here are three tips to avoid external distractions:

(i) **Learn to manage your emails.** Setting up filters, segregating emails according to projects and prioritizing them will save you several work hours every week. Beware of social networking sites—many people succumb to temptation and remain online even during working hours. Work all the time you work.

(ii) **Avoid making long phone calls.** The most common distraction during the working day is the phone call. Keep your conversations short and clear.

(iii) **Share your 'interruption time' with colleagues:** If you are working with a team, you can allocate a time during which your colleagues can interrupt you. Instead of having people approach you every now and then, you can let them know a time during the day, say between 3 and 4 p.m., when you are approachable.

(iv) **Drink plenty of water:** Fill up a water bottle at the start of the day and keep yourself hydrated. This will keep you healthy and save the time that you would otherwise spend on trips to the water cooler.

Do remember that no matter how hard you try, it is nearly impossible to completely get rid of distractions. So be ready to accept some interruptions at least.

'Obstacles are those frightening things you see when you take your eyes off your goal.'
—Henry Ford

Setting priorities

To use your time efficiently and enhance your focus, you must set your priorities in the right order. Be clear about the jobs that are urgent and those that can wait for the time being. Start by making a list of the jobs you need to do during the day and classify them under two priorities:

Priority I (Urgent jobs): Under this, place those tasks that demand your immediate attention. The best way to identify these jobs is to know where they are coming from. Urgent jobs are forced by external factors such as demands from your boss, your customers, telephone calls or emails, and requests from your family members, colleagues, etc. Try to finish these as quickly as possible. If you do not have a team to handle such issues, look for resourceful people around you and seek their help.

Priority II (Important jobs): These are where your skills matter the most. Allocate 'full focus' slots of thirty, sixty or ninety minutes to these tasks.

Remember, you must give more focus to important jobs and clear off the urgent ones quickly. If you are hard-pressed, bargain for more time to complete the urgent tasks or pass them on to somebody who can handle them as well as you can.

Use the 'Law of Forced Efficiency'

Young executives face great difficulty while focusing on work. You may have more than 200 hours of unfinished work on your desk. And the distractions may be innumerable. Here, you can apply the 'Law of Forced Efficiency'. This says that 'you will never have enough time to do everything but you will always have enough time to do the most important thing.' To apply this law, first make a list of everything you need to do during the day and then identify one or two of the most important things.

Once you know this, start work on the important things and focus all your attention on them. If there are interruptions or if some urgent tasks crop up, finish them quickly and return to the important jobs.

3. AN EMPOWERING EXERCISE TO UNLEASH THE POWER OF FOCUS WITHIN YOU

Imagine that the energy flowing in your mind and body is like a rough sea. Your soul is the ship sailing on this sea and your goal is the destination of this ship. To navigate on this rough sea, you must sail carefully or you are bound to get distracted. Fortunately, the Sea of Energy is under your control and so is the ship.

The challenge can be met if you first endeavour to control that Sea of Energy and then the ship. This way you can reach the destination with ease. Usually, people do it the opposite way. They try to take charge of the destination or attempt to control the ship in the rough sea. They do not realize that the sea, their energy, is also under their control. They keep working without realizing that they can control the energy that flows in and around them and that they have the power to use this energy to their advantage.

When you start focusing on one goal at a time without getting distracted, you trigger the 'Law of Attraction' which says that you attract things, people and circumstances corresponding to your positive thoughts. You can see this law in action right from the day you start applying it. To increase your focus and dramatically turn your life around, you must focus on the things you really want.

4. THE POWERFUL SYMBOL OF FOCUS

Dartboard: A dartboard is chosen as the symbol for the Power of Focus. It is a circular board with numbers on it. If you hit the centre, its bull's-eye. A dartboard tells you that you must concentrate all your attention on the centre and take action to hit the target. **See Figure 5.5**

The symbol of the Power of Focus

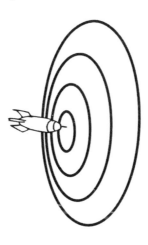

Dartboard

FIGURE 5.5

5. An Empowering Personality

How the Power of Focus empowered Lance Armstrong to fight cancer and win the world's toughest cycle race
Lance Armstrong is an American professional road-racing cyclist who won the Tour de France, one of the toughest tests in sports, a record-breaking seven consecutive times, from 1999 to 2005.

But even more stunning was his victory over testicular cancer, a tumor that metastasized to his brain and lungs in 1996. At that time, doctors said it was unlikely that he would live for more than a year. But instead of thinking about his disease, Armstrong focused on fighting back, surviving and winning. First, the doctors operated to remove the affected testicle and the lesions on his brain. Then they treated him with chemotherapy. Miraculously he recovered and, even more miraculously, came back to bike racing. What helped Armstrong all along was his Power of Focus. 'I decided I was going to win,' he said.

In 1997, Armstrong founded the Lance Armstrong Foundation, which supports people affected by cancer.

Three important lessons can be learnt from Armstrong's success:

i. Success is a long journey and during this journey you will often meet setbacks and frustration. Keep learning from these failures and move ahead without losing hope and enthusiasm.

ii. Focus on what you want.

iii. Choose to win and never give up.

6. EIGHT EMPOWERING QUESTIONS

   i. What am I doing today to increase my focus?

   ii. What is my highest-value task today?

   iii. Am I doing one thing at a time or trying to handle too many things?

   iv. Am I maintaining a daily list to complete the jobs in hand?

   v. How can I organize myself to give quality time to my important goals?

   vi. Am I focused on the work I have to complete today?

   vii. Is my determination enough to take me to my goal?

   viii. What will I look like when I have reached my goal?

7. EIGHT EMPOWERING AFFIRMATIONS

   i. I focus on the most important tasks every day and finish them.

   ii. I am clear about what I want.

   iii. I think about my goals and how I can achieve them, most of the time.

   iv. I maintain a to-do list and work on one thing at a time.

   v. I am a well-organized person and respect my time.

   vi. I write down one goal at a time on a piece of paper and work hard to achieve it.

   vii. I am determined to achieve all my goals.

   viii. I am learning new ways to improve my focus.

8. Eight tips to help you stay focused while working

1) **Work from a clear desk.** You cannot focus if you have too many things cluttered on your table. Remove all the files or papers from your table and move them to another table. Now bring one thing at a time in front of you, do it well and then go to the next.

2) **Do one thing at a time.** Multitasking is the great myth of the day. No one can multitask and remain 100 per cent efficient all the time. Our brain was not designed to think at multiple levels. You can do only one thing at a time. Once one task is done well, you can switch to the next and then the next. This alone can ensure that you deliver quality output.

3) **Plan and organize yourself.** Think of yourself as a highly organized person. Always keep a planner with you. Also keep a calendar on your desk. If anything new comes up that requires attention, make sure it is added to your to-do list.

4) **Allocate time slots for different activities.** Once you have made a list of things that are important, fix the amount of time you are going to spend in completing them.

5) **Do not switch between tasks.** Moving away from a task with the aim of returning to it later reduces your efficiency. Working single-mindedly and sticking to a task till it is complete will greatly increase your productivity.

6) **Avoid distractions during work.** To focus on work, try to eliminate distractions such as television, phone,

internet and email. Once this has been done, just you and your work remain.

7) **Use instrumental music.** Research has shown that music without lyrics helps increase focus at work. For me, having classical Indian and instrumental music playing in the background is a great help at work. Music with words and fast beats diverts my attention. You might have a different taste. So, pick and choose.

8) **Reward yourself.** Reward yourself once you finish even a small part of a big project. Have a cup of tea or coffee. This self-compliment will encourage you to move on to the next job with enthusiasm.

Success Principle #5:
Use the Power of Focus

Focus on what you want and on doing one thing at a time. The more you are able to focus on a task, the better you become and your chances of success increase.

Six
The Power of Will

1. UNDERSTANDING THE POWER OF WILL

'Conquer your weaknesses and fears, and you will conquer the world.'

—Shishir Srivastava

The secrets of heaven and hell

An old monk sat at the roadside. His eyes were closed, his legs crossed and his hands folded in his lap.

A samurai warrior disrupted his meditation and said, 'Old man, teach me about heaven and hell.'

At first, the monk did not respond. Gradually, he opened his eyes, the faintest hint of a smile playing around the corners of his mouth as the samurai waited impatiently.

'You wish to know the secrets of heaven and hell?' said the monk at last. 'You, who're so unkempt? You, whose hands and feet are covered with dirt? You, whose hair is uncombed, whose breath is foul, whose sword is all rusty and neglected? You, who're ugly and whose mother dresses you funny? You'll ask me of heaven and hell?'

The samurai uttered a vile curse. He drew his sword and raised it high above his head. His face turned crimson and the veins on his neck stood out in bold relief as he prepared to sever the monk's head from its shoulders.

'That is hell,' the monk said as the sword began its descent.

The samurai was overcome with amazement, awe, compassion and love for this gentle being who had risked his life to give him such a teaching. He stopped his sword in mid-flight and his eyes filled with grateful tears.

'And that,' said the monk, 'is heaven.'

—Father John W. Groff Jr

What is the Power of Will?

Will power is your inner strength to make decisions and act on them regardless of internal resistances. The Power of Will exists to help you cope with life's challenges. It drives you to attain goals or apply your talents irrespective of your emotional state.

It gives you the strength to overcome inertia and build momentum, and empowers you to get what you want by sticking to the job till it is done. Your Power of Will is strengthened whenever you reject instant gratification and instead choose to concentrate on something worthwhile.

The Power of Will helps you gather your energies and focus them in a positive direction. Let's say laziness prevents you from going on a planned morning walk. This is where you need to apply your Power of Will. This power can help you overcome bad habits such as overeating, laziness, procrastination and indiscipline.

> *'Be willing to be uncomfortable. Be comfortable being uncomfortable. It may get tough, but it's a small price to pay for living a dream.'*
>
> —Peter McWilliams

How the Power of Will helps you

When you develop an urge for self-improvement through your thoughts, words and deeds in pursuit of a higher goal, your Power of Will also develops. This power is a combined result of your firmness in sticking to decisions and persistence in moving towards your goals.

The Power of Will prospers when you develop the ability to control unnecessary and harmful impulses. It improves the ability to arrive at a decision and follow it through with perseverance until its successful completion. When you decide upon a list of things and behaviour that you will no longer accept from yourself, your decision-making ability grows and so does your willpower.

How to recognize your willpower

The Power of Will expands when you check your negative expressions in feeling, action or reaction. When you refuse to succumb to these unnecessary thoughts, you save energy. This energy gets stored for later use, when you want to do something more positive and constructive.

Three factors that affect the Power of Will

The three important factors that affect the development of your Power of Will are:

1) Self-discipline

2) Self-control

3) Self-determination

1) **Self-discipline** helps you do the right things in the right way at the right time, whether you like doing them or

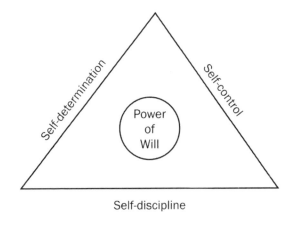

THE POWER OF WILL

FIGURE 6.1

not. It involves setting standards that you always adhere to. **See Figure 6.1**

Self-discipline helps you in achieving your goals

You are blessed with a free will; it is through self-discipline that you can train your will to overcome obstacles. Self-discipline may be used to lose weight, take up exercise or form a daily routine. It helps you persevere and rise above procrastination, laziness and indecisiveness. Self-discipline helps you respond to all tasks with the appropriate behaviour.

Self-discipline keeps you on the right track

Self-discipline helps you to minimize your mistakes by taking the right course of action at the right time. You can build self-discipline by gradually accepting challenges that allow you to perform beyond your comfort zone and help you reach the next level of success. The more you train yourself to be self-disciplined, the better you become. If you have been living your life with little discipline, do not set a tough routine for yourself in the beginning. Instead, resolve to make small improvements daily.

Self-discipline is a powerful tool to help you work for long hours

Some people see self-discipline as a 'cage' and worry that their creativity might 'die' if they try to discipline themselves. It is not so. Many great artists, musicians, singers and writers have succeeded by disciplining themselves to work for long hours at a stretch every day. They either burnt the midnight oil or got up early and worked all day long through self-mastery and self-discipline.

Self-discipline is an effective tool to reach your goals on time. It prevents you from excessive eating, smoking or any kind of obsessive behaviour. When you develop self-discipline, you become conscious of harmful inner impulses and gain the ability to reject them, realizing that they are not for your good. It might be difficult to practise self-discipline and it might seem that life becomes too dull and boring this way, but in the long run you will reap the benefits of the good habits you sow now.

Self-disciplined people:

- Are tough with themselves and stick to jobs till they are done
- Mind their own business and do not interfere in other people's business
- Keep a close watch over their actions
- Make a realistic daily routine and adhere to it

2) Self-control

This is the ability to keep a check over your internal universe—your thoughts and emotions—to gain control over your will and actions, which create the universe outside you.

According to an ancient Indian proverb, 'Before conquering the world, the king has to first conquer himself.' This holds true even today. To become successful, you must increase your Power of Will and exercise control over your thoughts, emotions, will and reactions. The more you can do this, the more successful you will become.

Self-control helps you to focus on your job

You are a treasure trove of energy and power. These can be best utilized when you stop succumbing to your cravings and whims. Once you start controlling unprofitable thoughts and become aware of the choices you make every day—even every hour—you start becoming more powerful from within.

Gain control over your senses

Once you have a clear picture of what you want to achieve, a whole new battle with the self starts. First, the senses that have been guiding your actions for years challenge you. They tend to pull you back the moment you begin a new battle. They divert your attention away from your goals and in different directions.

In the picture on this page, Lord Krishna is seen driving the chariot of Arjuna who is taking aim at the enemy (his target). The chariot is driven by four powerful horses (four negative emotions). Each animal has the potential to move in a direction of its choice. Lord Krishna is in control of the horses and guides them towards the enemy's forces.

Arjuna aiming at the target symbolizes you, a person who wants to accomplish a desired result. The four horses symbolize the powerful negative emotions of anger, lust, greed and pride. These emotions are the biggest hindrance in the fulfilment of your goals. But they can be replaced by positive emotions, when your senses are under control and become your friends in the journey towards success.

Later, Arjuna uses the Power of Will to conquer his emotions and regain his focus. He goes to the battlefield and with only a handful of soldiers on his side defeats the enemy's huge army. He emerges as a great warrior, symbolizing the victory of good over evil.

Similarly, you too have the Power of Will on your side in the battle against your negative emotions. Your goal is to defeat these negative emotions with positive ones.

> *'You are what you are when you are alone and you become what you choose.'*
> —**Shishir Srivastava**

People who practise self-control do things with punctuality and orderliness. They manage themselves well and mind their own business. They conduct themselves properly and guard their thoughts and actions. They set the right example and keep a strict watch over their actions.

Through self-control, you can:

- Gain personal mastery over your life
- Eliminate the feeling of helplessness and being too dependent on others
- Become a trustworthy and responsible human being
- Develop a strong sense of self-esteem and self-confidence

. . . and keep a check over:

- Uncontrolled emotional responses such as anger, dissatisfaction, unhappiness, resentment and fear
- Self-destructive, addictive, obsessive and impulsive behaviour

- The urge to criticize people behind their backs

3) Self-determination

This is your decision-making ability.

Self-determination helps you to stick to your resolutions

Maybe you have tried to change your eating habits but failed to do so because of a lack of inner strength and persistence. Most people have had such an experience.

Once you have determined to shun laziness and take control of your emotions, you will develop the ability to stick to your resolutions. You are born to be rich, famous, successful, happy and healthy. If you have fallen short on any of these counts, it only means that you need to examine the state of your spiritual orientation. Your inner voice will guide you towards the right path. You must listen to your feelings, notice what is working and what is not. Resolve to change your life. Self-determination is the vital first step.

Self-determination takes you towards self-improvement

Some people think it is enough to work hard to succeed. Although this is true to some extent, your performance at a task will not improve unless you work hard on yourself too. All work—be it that of a student, a doctor, an actor, a businessman or a worker in an office—becomes much easier when people start focusing on self-improvement.

For at least half an hour a day, read about successful people in your field and try to find out what helped them achieve success. Then try to inculcate those qualities in yourself.

Self-determination leads to inner strength

Self-determination gives you the inner strength to aim at a goal and take action irrespective of discomfort, difficulty or unwillingness from within. It is the inner power that helps you overcome your emotional resistance to taking action.

Self-determination helps you to:

• Stick to your resolutions till you meet your goals

• Work on continuous self-improvement

• Develop your inner strength

2. HOW TO DEVELOP YOUR POWER OF WILL

All highly successful people possess tons of willpower. So do you. Training and exercising your willpower develops strength, courage and assertiveness. The only person you have to win over in this world is yourself and your will helps you do just that. Here are some ways to strengthen your willpower:

Become self-disciplined

While practising self-discipline, you have to be realistic and precise in what you want to achieve. You cannot expect results overnight. To build discipline in any area—say, work, communication or managing finances—you must know where you stand right now. You can only start from here.

Improve your self-control

You must exercise self-control to gain full mastery over yourselves so that all your actions lead towards your goals.

In the film *Pumping Iron*, Arnold Schwarzenegger reveals

how he won the Mr Universe title for five consecutive years. One night before a final event, Schwarzenegger's mother called to tell him that his father had died. Schwarzenegger was utterly devastated but kept his emotions in control and decided to give the title his best shot to honour his father. He won but could not attend his father's funeral. Asked how he felt about this incident and what kept him going, Schwarzenegger said, *'To be successful, you have to keep complete control over your emotions, or they will control you.'*

The downside of losing self-control. France took on Italy in the 2006 FIFA World Cup final. Both teams scored within the first twenty minutes, but the game remained tied at the end of regulation time. During extra-time, the French captain Zinadine Zidane, playing his last game before retirement, lost control over his emotions and headbutted an Italian player. Zidane was shown the red card and had to leave the field. France went on to lose the final.

Zidane lost control over himself and gave way to his anger. The Italian player must have soon recovered from his injury, but Zidane will never be able to forget his moment of madness.

'Either you control your attitude or it controls you.'
—**Anonymous**

When you don't exert control over your emotions, you lose your powers. No matter how bad the situation 'outside' may be, you can always control your 'inside' universe with patience. Whenever your emotions become too dominant, say to yourself, *'Be patient, be patient, be patient.'* Whoever can control their emotions can control the world. Self-control develops when you show the willingness to follow your chosen path.

A good way to know the direction in which you are going is to observe the course of your thoughts. If your thoughts are proceeding in a negative direction, you need to check them and move them to a positive direction. Start thinking positively whenever you are confronted with negative thoughts, and repeat positive affirmations to yourself. Positive feelings such as joy, enthusiasm and love make for a pleasant personality and also win the attention of positive people.

> *'Three great essentials to achieve anything worthwhile are, first, hard work; second, stick-to-it-iveness; third, common sense.'*
> —Thomas Edison

Never blame others if you do something wrong

The best way to keep yourself empowered is to accept the responsibility for all your actions. When something goes wrong, get busy in finding out the cause of the problem and how you can prevent it from happening again in the future. Learn to acknowledge your mistakes and do so before someone else points them out. This will also help you get a good night's sleep.

Successful people take full charge of themselves and assume total responsibility for their actions.

How to develop strong self-determination

There are two major weaknesses that lead to inaction and stand as a huge obstacle before us on the road to success. They are:

i) Procrastination

ii) Laziness

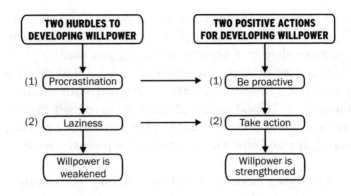

FIGURE 6.2

If you observe carefully, you will discover that these two weaknesses are interconnected and one leads to the other. If you do not make a clear decision, you will fall prey to procrastination, which, in turn, will lead to laziness.

i) Moving from procrastination to pro-action

Many people avoid doing work because they think it can be done later or they can get away by not doing it. Such an attitude gives rise to the habit of procrastination. This habit can take hold of people to the extent that even the thought of making a phone call or writing down daily goals becomes a burden. While action breeds accomplishment, inaction breeds procrastination and laziness. **See Figure 6.2**

Four steps to overcome procrastination:

Step 1: *Acknowledge the problem.*
Step 2: *Get clarity about the work.*
Step 3: *Visualize yourself doing the work.*
Step 4: *Take action.*

Step 1: *Acknowledge the problem*

If you have developed the procrastination habit, the first thing you need to do is to acknowledge it. Accept that you have picked up a bad habit. Now take charge and tell yourself, 'Instead of just sitting idle or procrastinating about this job again, I will do something about it.'

Step 2: *Get clarity about the work*

Tell yourself that the work you have been delaying is the most important one before you. Get rid of all the thoughts and actions that are not associated with this task. Make a list of all the important things you need to do in order to complete this work.

Step 3: *Visualize yourself doing the work*

Take a few deep breaths and close your eyes. Think about this task and visualize yourself doing it. Think of each step as an important one. Just as a recipe is not complete till all the ingredients are there, your job requires all the elements to fall in place.

Step 4: *Take action*

Close your eyes again and take twenty quick deep breaths. This will pump in extra oxygen and make your brain more active. Open your eyes and get down to work. Do one thing at a time and then switch over to the next. Act with faith and keep telling yourself, 'Yes, I can do it.' Soon you will discover that your work is done.

> *'Putting off an easy thing makes it hard. Putting off a hard thing makes it impossible.'*
> —Charles Wilson

ii) Overcoming laziness and becoming active

a) *Why laziness?*

Laziness is an attitude which starts with thoughts of inaction. It is a combined result of indecisiveness and procrastination. Mostly, laziness is only a mental phenomenon and shapes an attitude. It is inaction at the place of action. It is giving space to procrastination where you are required to be proactive.

Aristotle once said, '*Lazy is not only he who doesn't work but also he who knows he can do it better and yet doesn't do that.*'

First, we nurture this bad habit by putting off things until tomorrow. Though all jobs on your list cannot be completed in a day, do not put off the small tasks that can be easily done today.

If laziness has prevented you from taking action to fulfil your goals, begin by acknowledging the fact. Then get physically active by doing some mild exercises. Just move your hands, shake your body, put on some lively music or go for a walk. As you get your body moving, it will become more alert and prepare itself to respond to your mind's instructions. Our muscles and nervous system are not separate entities. They respond to each other's requests. Some scientists even believe we have a 'second brain' in our gut—and the phrase 'gut feeling' seems to suggest as much.

b) *Get out of your comfort zone*

Many a time you avoid hard work thinking you have had enough for the day and nothing else is required of you. It is then that you start seeking pleasure and trying to avoid things that are painful. Your aim should be to get out of this comfort zone and maintain a balance between pain and pleasure. Too much of either can stall your progress.

My Comfort Zone

I used to have a comfort zone where I knew I wouldn't fail.
The same four walls and busywork were really more like jail.
I longed so much to do the things I'd never done before,
But stayed inside my comfort zone and paced the same old floor.
I said it didn't matter that I wasn't doing much.
I said I didn't care for things like commission checks and such.
I claimed to be so busy with the things inside the zone,
But deep inside I longed for something special of my own.
I couldn't let my life go by just watching others win.
I held my breath; I stepped outside and let the change begin.
I took a step and with new strength I'd never felt before,
I kissed my comfort zone goodbye and closed and locked the
    door.
If you're in a comfort zone, afraid to venture out,
Remember that all winners were at one time filled with doubt.
A step or two and words of praise can make your dreams
    come true.
Reach for your future with a smile; success is there for you!
                                                            —Anonymous

3. AN EMPOWERING EXERCISE TO UNLEASH THE POWER OF WILL WITHIN YOU

Identify a weakness within you that you would like to overcome. It could be a habit that has developed over a period of time such as procrastination, laziness or irritability. Your job in this exercise is to overcome your weakness and make it your strength through the Power of Will. Here we will try to overcome procrastination.

Close your eyes, feel the immense energy flowing around you and feel that you are in full control of this energy. Do some fast breathing and visualize doing something which excites you but which you have been dragging your feet over. After about ten rapid breaths and with a relaxed mind, see that all this energy gets concentrated at one place, in the centre of your mind, and believe that you can use this power to perform the job you have been postponing.

Now open your eyes, get up and take ONE STEP to do what you just visualized. Do something to achieve it, however small the step may be. It can be making a phone call, writing an instruction to a junior, leaving a note at your desk or feeding a reminder into your cellphone. Use your power to do something in the direction of achieving your goal. Take that one tiny step, just do it, and you will feel a great power unleashing within you.

Your ONE small, yet POWERFUL step will take you closer to your goal. It will increase your power within seconds and boost your self-confidence. Now, you are all set to give a new shape to your universe.

Someone rightly said, 'It is the ACT of taking the FIRST STEP that separates a winner from a loser.' So Act, Act, ACT NOW!

4. THE POWERFUL SYMBOL OF THE POWER OF WILL

Earth: Earth is chosen as the symbol of the Power of Will as it keeps revolving with persistence and never stops. Days, months, seasons and years roll by, but the earth keeps going round and round—and has been doing so for millions of years. You too have the Power of Will like the Earth. We all are travelling around the sun, yet we hardly feel the earth's movement. Similarly, the power driving our life from inside is our will. The more attention you pay to developing your willpower, the better your life will be. **See Figure 6.3**

The symbol of the Power of Will

Earth

FIGURE 6.3

5. AN EMPOWERING PERSONALITY

How the Power of Will inspired Kiran Bedi to choose a challenging career and succeed
    Kiran Bedi was the first woman to join the Indian Police Service (IPS) in 1972. One of the country's most admired and widely known police officers, she retired in 2007.
    At one time she used to be popularly known as 'Crane Bedi'—for having towed away Prime Minister Indira Gandhi's car for a parking violation. (Gandhi was on a visit to the United States.) During her career, Bedi influenced

several decisions of the IPS, particularly in the areas of traffic management, VIP security and the fight against narcotics.

From 1993 to 1995 Bedi was posted as inspector general of prisons at Tihar Jail, one of world's largest prison complexes. During that time, she initiated a number of reform measures such as detoxification programmes for prisoners, yoga sessions, vipassana meditation and literacy drives.

Bedi believes her willpower and desire to excel helped her beat the odds throughout her career. Today, she is an inspiration for millions in India.

Three important lessons can be learnt from Bedi's life:

a) The Power of Will can help you see through the tough phases in life.

b) Willpower develops the consistency that is essential to achieve goals.

c) Through the Power of Will you can differentiate between right and wrong, and choose the best path for success.

6. EIGHT EMPOWERING QUESTIONS

i. Am I focused on my goal? What can I do to increase my concentration?

ii. What new challenges do I have to face today and how am I prepared to meet them?

iii. How am I organizing my daily schedule to achieve maximum impact today?

iv. While I am working hard to achieve my goal, am I prepared to persist till the end?

v. What steps am I taking to ensure that I am in full control of my emotional state?

vi. What new behaviours am I adapting today to develop my willpower?

vii. How am I developing my inner strength?

viii. What old behaviours, which have been keeping me down, am I rejecting today?

7. EIGHT EMPOWERING AFFIRMATIONS

i. I focus on my goals and live each day with passion and power.

ii. I enjoy life's challenges and learn from everything that happens in my life.

iii. I'm successful because I have a disciplined attitude towards life.

iv. I'm willing to put in my best to achieve my goals. I feel powerful and excited when I do so.

v. I'm controlling my destiny today and am growing stronger in my abilities.

vi. My willpower is increasing every day and I feel I am the master of every situation I face.

vii. I have tremendous confidence in my talents and abilities.

viii. I am able to control my negative emotions and feelings every time they threaten to control me.

8. EIGHT TIPS TO HELP YOU ENHANCE YOUR WILL

1) **Keep a check over your negative emotions.** Negative energies will try to pull you down like gravity. They may draw your attention to minor things and distract

you from your real goals. So, beware of them and remain focused on your larger goals.

2) **Take responsibility and develop your powers.** It is rightly said, 'With greater power comes greater responsibility.' It seems that all powers are expressed so that you gather more control over yourself and act with responsibility. When you do this, you will find that success and happiness will come easily to you.

3) **If you have a choice to be easy or tough with yourself, choose the latter.** The centre of control is inside your brain and when you learn how to gain control over this centre, you become the master of your destiny. To do so, you have to be a bit tough upon yourself to begin with. Life has a simple equation: if you are easy with yourself today, life is going to be tough on you tomorrow, but if you are going to be tough with yourself today, life will be easy for you tomorrow.

4) **An empowering exercise.** Whenever you are free, find something that you would like to do or that has been pending for a long time. If you are at a railway station, bus stop or anyplace where you are required to wait, try to be proactive. Use the time to review your goals list, make a phone call or send an email. Make use of your free time.

5) **Reject instant gratification.** If you see an ice-cream parlour while walking down a street and are tempted to have your favourite flavour, do not give in to temptation. This way you will learn how to postpone gratification.

6) **Do the essential work first.** If you have something important to do, make sure you do not procrastinate.

Finish the task first—sticking to it until it is complete. Control the desire to go out for a dinner, a film or a party with a friend.

7. **Clean up the dirt.** If there is a corner in your house that needs to be cleaned or if some books have to be arranged on a shelf, do not let laziness hold you back. When you come back home tired, instead of switching on the TV, take a bath and revitalize yourself.

8. **Get physically active.** If you have choice between climbing the stairs or taking the elevator, choose the stairs.

Success Principle #6:
Use the Power of Will

Develop your willpower by using self-determination and self-discipline to keep a check over your negative emotions, and do what is necessary.

Seven
The Power of Action

1. UNDERSTANDING THE POWER OF ACTION

'Every morning in Africa, a gazelle wakes up.
It knows it must run faster than the fastest lion or it
will be killed.
Every morning in Africa, a lion wakes up.
It knows it must outrun the gazelle or it will starve to death.
It doesn't matter whether you are a lion or a gazelle,
When the sun comes up, you'd better be running.'
—*A quote hung up in basketball great Michael Jordan's room*

'I've missed more than 9,000 shots in my career. I've lost almost 300 games. Twenty-six times, I've been trusted to take the game-winning shot and missed. I've failed over and over and over again in my life. And that's why I succeed.'

—Michael Jordan

Defining action

Action means converting your thoughts into a physical reality through consistent effort. It is putting things in motion and getting them done. To 'act' is to work on your thoughts to achieve your goals.

The pot of success

You can imagine your ultimate success to be a pot that has to be built and filled. With the powers of Imagination, Words, Self-Confidence, Goal Setting, Focus and Will you have strengthened this pot and given it a beautiful shape. Now the pot is ready and shining from the outside, but it will remain empty without action. People will come and appreciate this beautiful and strong pot from afar but when they come near it, they will find it empty. Through your Power of Action you will decide how quickly you fill this pot. **See Figure 7.1**

'We should be taught not to wait for inspiration to start a thing. Action always generates inspiration. Inspiration seldom generates action.'

—Frank Tibolt

How the Power of Action is born

Every action that you take is the result of a desire that resides deep within your heart. If your intentions are good and you

THE POT OF SUCCESS
(Empty without action)

THE POT OF SUCCESS
(Full with action)

The pot of success can be strengthened and given a beautiful shape through the powers of imagination, words, self-confidence, goal setting, focus and will, but it takes a lot of action to fill it.

THE POWER OF ACTION

FIGURE 7.1

are clear about what you want to achieve, you are already halfway to success. It is the Power of Action that will take you through the next half. What is required is firm faith in yourself and a clearly defined purpose. The Power of Action is born in your heart as you aim for your goal with a strong will.

You have the seed of greatness inside you

We all know that a seed cannot become a tree in one day. Every seed has an inherent capacity to grow but it needs a caring gardener who will plant it in the correct environment and take care of it with patience until it grows into a tree. Similarly, your soul has the potential to embrace the universe around you and give shape to your dreams, ambitions and desires. All you need is to act like the caring gardener of your mind, body and soul.

'We have to understand that the world can only be grasped by action, not by contemplation. The hand is more important than the eye . . . The hand is the cutting edge of the mind.'
—Jacob Bronowski

Action is a natural process

Growth is a natural process. A seed becomes a sapling with natural ease. Does it make any special effort to grow? Certainly not.

Once you start following the simple steps mentioned in this chapter, you will be able to tap the secret of setting things in motion with the least effort. Most people do not take action because they think it is painful to act. But they forget an important fact: everything in the universe is in constant motion in some form or the other. Each and every cell of your body and each atom of the universe is in motion. So taking action is something that you do in harmony with the universe.

Coordination with the least effort

The human body is a classic example of coordination with the least effort. Innumerable living cells perform individual actions but they work together to ensure that the body works smoothly. Your heart, for example, beats over one lakh times a day; yet you are probably not aware how effectively it functions. The same goes for the brain, the liver and many other organs. In a larger sense, our body is the perfect example of great teamwork. Similarly, when you use the Power of Action and have a clear goal, all your body parts fall into a rhythm to achieve the target.

2. How to Develop Your Power of Action

To activate the Power of Action from within, you need to follow a three-step process:

Step 1: Get started.

Step 2: See yourself as a highly organized and productive person.

Step 3: Persist till you achieve your goal.

Step 1: Get started

a) *Get your priorities right*

As Stephen Covey says in *First Things First*: 'The Main Thing is to keep the Main Thing the Main Thing.' Focus your powers on what is most important to you rather than squander them on non-essentials. Once you set your priorities, take action in that order.

b) *A step-by-step process should be adopted to do a great job*

The gap between your present situation and the fulfilment of your goal can be bridged only through the Power of Action. It is a step-by-step process, not a long jump. Many wonderful ideas and plans conceived by philosophers, scientists and intelligent people come to nothing because of the lack of sustained effort. While working on the job in hand, keep your attention focused on your ultimate objective. **See Figure 7.2**

c) *Don't wait for perfect conditions to start working*

Most outstanding achievers have worked in adverse conditions and emerged victorious. For example, Michael

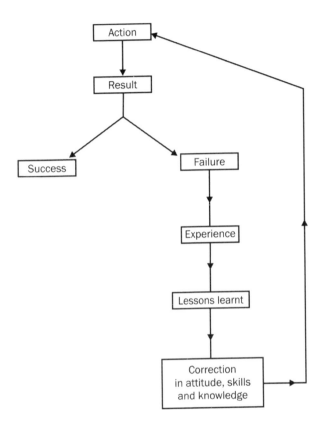

FIGURE 7.2

Jordan was declared unfit for his high school basketball team. He had a choice. He could either lock himself up in his room or look himself in the mirror and resolve to take action in the pursuit of his dreams. He chose the latter—and went on to become one of the world's best basketball players.

The universe is not perfect—it is as it should be. So you too shouldn't wait for things to be perfect before you start. You have to simply act on one thing at a time and move on to the next task. If you are thinking of starting your own business or company, you don't have to wait for the funds to be there or for the resources to be at your disposal to take the first step. Start by doing whatever is available to you and never let what you can't do stop you from doing what you can do.

d) *Use the trial-error-succeed method*

How many attempts did you make to just stand up and walk when you were a toddler? Three? Four? Ten? More? For most of you the answer would be much more than ten. But you didn't give up. Success often comes after a person has failed many times in his efforts. After failing to climb Mount Everest in two attempts, Edmond Hillary said, 'I will come again and conquer you, for you as a mountain cannot grow but I as a human being can.' He did just that in his third attempt and became the first person to scale Mount Everest.

We tend to forget the important trial-error-succeed method we mastered while learning essential activities such as walking or riding a bike in childhood. Always remember that the secret of success is 'inside' us. See **Figure 7.3**

Most people give up after the first few unsuccessful attempts and develop a fear of failure. They then associate this fear with the shame of being criticized by the people around them. This need not be the case. You will pass through four stages on your way to becoming a true winner:

- **First:** People will make fun of you when you start your efforts. If you persist . . .

FOUR STEPS TO OUTSTANDING SUCCESS

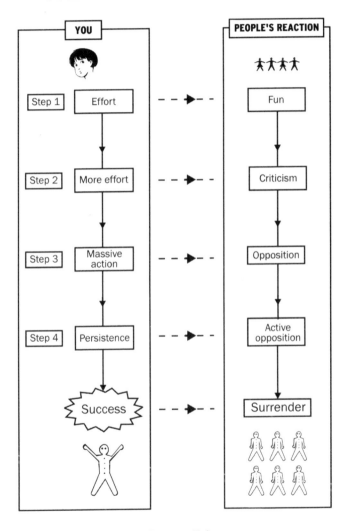

FIGURE 7.3

- **Second:** . . . people will start criticizing you. If you still keep on going . . .

- **Third:** . . . people will actively oppose you. If you keep hanging on and stay determined . . .

- **Fourth:** . . . people will finally give up and let you go ahead with what you have been doing, and you will finally emerge triumphant. **See Figure 7.4**

Four steps to unleash the Power of Action from within you:

STEP 1	GET STARTED!
STEP 2	SET GOALS
STEP 3	STAY FOCUSED
STEP 4	BE PERSISTENT

FIGURE 7.4

So you don't have to be worried about mockery, criticism or opposition. You do not have any control over these negative reactions of people and you should not react to them. When the Wright Brothers were attempting to make an aeroplane, most people believed that 'human beings cannot fly, otherwise we would have being given wings.' But the Wright Brothers persisted, went ahead with their experiments and finally succeeded.

Ignore what people say. Instead, focus on the main goal. The only control you can exercise is upon your emotions. So do something that makes you feel good. Listen to some heart-throbbing music or take part in an activity you enjoy—say, painting, running, playing the piano. Or simply get down to work.

e) *Be unique, follow the road less travelled*

The wise thing to do is to create a new path for yourself and be an original person. If you follow the footprints of others, how will you create your own? Mahatma Gandhi said, 'I will not follow the beaten track.' Instead of propagating the idea of a violent revolt against the British Empire, he created his own path of non-violence.

> *'The important thing is to explore what everyone has achieved and then start from there!'*
> —**Shishir Srivastava**

f) *Act realistically*

You must act in a realistic way, taking life and people *as they are* and not as you want them to be. Realistic people are constantly working to make things happen since they have visualized them happening.

You will have to work to develop the character and traits of a realistic person while you handle pressure conditions. Be calm, confident and constructive in difficult times. If you can do so, you will emerge victorious and be a source of inspiration for many others.

g) *Persist with your Power of Action*

You may have worked long and hard on a task and yet failed to make much progress. Still, remember that no defeat is permanent till you accept it as reality and quit trying. All your attempts help to build your 'preparatory muscles'—the muscles that prepare you to succeed—and make your desire, faith and commitment stronger. Once your have built the right muscles, you will succeed with the least effort. When you remain persistent, your Power of Action develops.

Sometimes things do not work for you because you have been trying to work on circumstances that are 'outside' you and hence beyond your control. What you need to do is work hard upon yourself to express the eight powers within you.

Some magic seems to work for people who keep on trying. Such people remain persistent and a day comes when the universe finally reveals to them the secret of success. Edison failed 10,000 times in his attempts to invent the first light bulb. But he finally succeeded. American athlete Wilma Rudolph, who had polio at the age of six, was told by her mother that one day she would not only walk but also run. Rudolph proved her mother right when she won three gold medals in track and field events in the 1960 Rome Olympics.

> *'Never, never, never give up.'*
>
> —Winston Churchill

Plan your act and act your plan

Make a comprehensive list of all the resources needed and all the actions required to achieve your goal. Then divide your major goal into small sub-goals. Instead of worrying about making a precise plan, make a quick 'to-do' list on paper and start working on one thing at a time. Get going.

> *'Whatever you can do, or dream you can, begin it. Boldness has genius, power and magic in it.'*
>
> —Goethe

Step 2: See yourself as a highly organized and productive person

To enhance your performance, you must see yourself as an efficient person who is highly organized and productive. For this, you must:

a) *Set a deadline*

If you aren't making progress fast enough, look at the sub-goals and set a deadline for each one. This will help you to decide which goals need to be given priority. You will also be able to put power behind your goals as your subconscious mind will focus more on the jobs that have deadlines attached.

b) *Become efficient and productive*

Successful people are highly productive and keep reminding themselves of the end result they want to achieve. They practise effective time-management techniques, build upon their strengths and cut down their weaknesses. Their power lies in their ability to make decisions, stick to them and work till the desired results are obtained.

> *'Begin doing what you want to do now. We have only this moment, sparkling like a star in our hand—and melting like a snowflake.'*
> —Marie Beyon Ray

c) *Use your creative thinking to solve problems*

As you grow personally and professionally while using the Power of Action, you will realize that most of your time will be spent in solving problems. The process of problem solving can be energy draining or fun depending upon your attitude.

Albert Einstein said, 'We cannot solve the problem with the same level of thinking that created it.' Therefore, you must rise above the level of the problem to solve it. If you consider all problems as opportunities to develop your creative potential and treat them as puzzles to be solved by action, life will become more fun. It's about perceiving the situation with a positive attitude.

> *'If one ADVANCES confidently in the direction of his dreams, and endeavours to live the life that he has imagined, he WILL meet with success unexpected in common hours.'*
>
> —Henry David Thoreau

Step 3: Be persistent to achieve your goal

The universe tests our intensity of desire till the last step and those who maintain a never-give-up attitude ultimately succeed. You must develop a similar attitude. You need a strong commitment to finish the job from start to finish. Just as water does not turn to steam even if it is boiled to 99.9 degrees centigrade—it needs to be heated up to a full 100 degrees centigrade— you too can't get away by doing only 99.9 per cent of the job. You must give your 100 per cent to it and persist till the task is accomplished.

Do more than you are paid for

All peak performers agree that their success was the result of always doing more than they were paid for. These highly productive people make it a habit of working hard and giving their best shot to every task assigned to them. Result: they are given additional responsibilities and they get promoted faster. They also get paid more.

Use the momentum principle

According to the 'Momentum Principle of Success' it takes a lot of energy to get into action mode and keep moving but it takes far less energy to keep moving once you have started. All successful people are busy people because the momentum is with them and they do not want to break it.

Work hard and stay on the job till it is complete

According to an article in the *Fortune* magazine, many CEOs of Fortune 500 corporations were not too talented in school. But they still reached great heights of success through hard work and determination. Thomas Edison, the greatest inventor ever born, was expelled from school when he was in the sixth grade. But he went on to become a super achiever on the basis of his perseverance and commitment towards work.

> *'Perseverance is a positive, active characteristic. It is not idly, passively waiting and hoping for some good thing to happen. It gives us hope by helping us realize that the righteous suffer no failure except in giving up and no longer trying. We must never give up, regardless of temptations, frustrations, disappointments or discouragements.'*
>
> —Joseph B. Wirthlin

3. An empowering exercise to unleash the power of Action within you

Set this book aside for a moment and take a walk inside your room. Think what more you can do to achieve your goals and write it down. This will put every cell of your body on high alert. Your whole being will start contributing towards helping you achieve your purpose.

To get physically active (if you do not exercise regularly), you can start by walking for 10 to 15 minutes each day for a week. Gradually add five minutes after every week till you have a daily walking schedule of 30 minutes. Try and maintain this standard and you will see how active you can remain throughout the day. This will help you to build your stamina, strength and gradually your speed of working.

4. The Powerful Symbol of Action

Woodpecker: The woodpecker is a classic example of the Power of Action. It keeps boring into tree barks with its small beak and gradually manages to cut hard wood into small

The symbol of the Power of Action

Woodpecker

Figure 7.5

pieces. The bird drills with perseverance, knowing it will eventually succeed in making a hole. This is how the Power of Action can overcome a seemingly huge obstacle with continuous efforts. See Figure 7.5

5. AN EMPOWERING PERSONALITY

How the Power of Action helped Dhirubhai Ambani *rise from rags to riches, and set up India's largest corporate house*

Dhirubhai Ambani (1932–2002) was the founder chairman of Reliance Industries Limited, India's largest private-sector organization. From a humble beginning as the son of a village teacher in Gujarat, he went on to create a multi-billion dollar business empire within just 25 years.

Ambani's corporate philosophy was short and simple: *'Think big. Think differently. Think fast. Think ahead. Aim for the best.'* When it came to action, he was always quick. The Bhagavad Gita says, *'The actions of a great man are an inspiration for others. Whatever he does becomes a standard for others to follow.'*

Ambani was an exceptional human being and an outstanding leader. He dared to dream on an unimaginable scale. His life and achievements prove that backed by confidence, courage and conviction, a person can achieve the impossible. The $125-billion (about Rs 575,000 crore) Reliance Group is a living testimony to his indomitable will and single-minded commitment to his goals. He dedicated himself to meeting all his goals through the Power of Action.

Three important lessons can be learnt from Ambani's life:

a) Action leads to the realization of goals and dreams.

b) One must think and act on a large scale. This helps transform dreams into reality.

c) One small action can start a process that can help you achieve your goals faster than you thought was possible.

6. EIGHT EMPOWERING QUESTIONS

i. How can I divide my bigger goals into smaller ones so that I act on one thing at a time?

ii. Have I started doing what I have decided?

iii. How quickly and how well can I get this task done?

iv. How am I maximizing my output?

v. What is the ultimate objective of my goals?

vi. What is helping me to achieve this goal?

vii. What actions can I take right now that will help me to move forward?

viii. What are the essential steps that I need to take to finish my work?

7. EIGHT EMPOWERING AFFIRMATIONS

i. Whenever I act, I do so positively and enthusiastically.

ii. I believe that self-improvement is a continuous process. Therefore I keep learning, unlearning and relearning.

iii. Whenever an urgent task comes up, I try to do it immediately.

iv. I act with confidence and hope that all my actions taken towards reaching my goals will be successful.

v. Whenever I face a challenging task, I sit down calmly and divide it into small tasks, prioritize these tasks and then work upon them one at a time.

vi. I'm making the most of my life now and every day.

vii. I keep my focus on the work in hand.

viii. I have a sense of urgency and try to finish all my jobs on time.

8 EIGHT TIPS TO HELP YOU ENHANCE THE POWER OF YOUR ACTIONS

1) **Act with positive feelings.** Take action in the direction of your goals with courage, confidence and conviction. When you do so, results will start showing up sooner or later. Also, others will start seeing you as a charismatic person.

2) **Learn and improve continuously through the Power of Action.** You stand here today because this is where your thoughts and education have brought you. To progress further you need to bring about a paradigm shift in your thoughts and actions through an investment in self-improvement. Do something to improve yourself daily: take a walk and talk to yourself positively, record your voice with positive auto-suggestions, read motivational quotes, or just plan your day and work accordingly.

3) **Develop the habit of doing things 'now'.** Adopt the golden habit of doing things 'now'. This way you will

gain confidence, win control over situations and ultimately become the master of your destiny. Remember that not doing a thing and thinking that you will do it later is more painful than just doing it now.

4) **Act on your thoughts.** All successful people have the habit of converting their thoughts into some form of action as soon as possible. To be successful, try to bring your thoughts out of your mind. Write them down, be clear about what you want and then take action on your thoughts.

5) **Follow a step-by-step process.** Growth is a step-by-step process and it should be kept that way. While taking action, you might become impatient, but remember that there are no shortcuts to success. So, discipline yourself and be prepared for a long haul.

6) **Divide your daily goals into small parts.** The best way to avoid procrastination is to divide a big job into small doable parts. This will help you focus on one part of the work at a time and take action. Once a small part is done, you should move to the next and then to the next and so on. This way you will gain momentum and the work will not seem daunting.

7) **A mantra for action.** Sometimes trivial distractions come in the way of doing something important. Suppose you have decided to devote one hour to self-improvement but find your attention being diverted by a film that your family is watching. What should you do? Remind yourself that your goal is more important than this film. The film can be watched at leisure but the goal has a time limit. To get your focus back to work, say to yourself, 'Do it now. Do it now. Do it now.'

8) **Get excited about your job.** Success and happiness follow positive action, and more positive action follows success and happiness. Successful people are always excited and enthusiastic about their profession—and they work hard at it. When you complete a task, no matter how small or big it might be, your brain releases endorphins which make you feel elated and excited. It is the brain's way of telling you, 'Well done, keep it up!' The better you perform a task, the more your Power of Action will develop.

Success Principle #7:
Use the Power of Action

Do most of the time what you would like to do the most. Stick with steadfastness to your goals and take constant action to accomplish them, come what may. Also take out time to assess 'where you are from' and 'where you have to go'.

Eight
The Power of Love

1. UNDERSTANDING THE POWER OF LOVE

Tale of two brothers

Two brothers worked together on their family farm. One was married and had a large family. The other was single. At the day's end, the brothers shared their produce and profits equally.

One day, the single brother said to himself, 'It's not right that we should share the produce and profits equally. I'm alone and my needs are simple.' So each night, he would take a sack of grain from his bin, cross the field between their houses and dump the sack into his brother's bin.

Meanwhile, the married brother said to himself, 'It's not right that we should share the produce and profits equally. After all, I'm married and have my wife and children to look after me in the years to come. My brother has no one to take care of his future.' So each night he would take a sack of grain and dump it into his single brother's bin.

Both men remained puzzled for years because their supply of grain never dwindled. Then one night the brothers bumped into each other and the penny dropped. They let go of their sacks and embraced one another.

What is love?

Love is the unifying power in the universe that helps us attain our true purpose. It is an emotion associated with warmth, joy, giving, sharing, compassion, gratitude, belongingness, spirit of service and forgiveness. From the tiny particles in an atom to the mighty stars in galaxies, love binds everything in the universe. Here we are talking about the pure, unconditional love that lies deep in our heart and is the source of infinite power.

> '*A human being is a part of the whole that we call the universe, a part limited in time and space. He experiences himself, his thoughts and feelings, as something separated from the rest—a kind of optical illusion of his consciousness. This illusion is a prison for us, restricting us to our personal desires and to affection for only the few people nearest us. Our task must be to free ourselves from this prison by widening*

> *our circle of compassion to embrace all living beings*
> *and all of nature.'*
>
> —Albert Einstein

Unconditional love

The term 'love' is frequently used to describe the strong feeling of affection between lovers. On the other hand, 'unconditional love' is used to portray love between family members, friends and between others in committed relationships. When you love someone regardless of their actions or beliefs, you express unconditional love.

True love is unconditional love towards one and all. Like the sun's rays, it is warm; like rose petals, it adds colour and joy to life; like a mountain stream, it flows freely and encircles all creation.

The reason people tend to express anger, confusion and resentment is because of the lack of unconditional love. Our emotional need for unconditional love is like our physical need for food and air. Where unconditional love is missing, people tend to behave in an abnormal way and tend to adopt violent and aggressive means to gain attention.

Giving without any expectations

Unconditional love is giving love without any condition or expectation in return. Once we love others in true spirit, we strike a chord with the universe and radiate the positive energy of love from within us, like the sun. Also like the sun, the Power of Love thrives on itself. When we radiate true love, we receive true love in return.

When you start loving all life on earth with an equal eye, you generate a strong sense of interconnection with everything. Since we all thrive on common resources such as food, air, shelter and water, we share a strong connection with each and every being. Thus, the Power of Love is always available to us. You can tap this potential by cultivating a heart that gives and receives without expectations.

> 'We make a living by what we get;
> we make a life by what we give.'
> —Sir Winston Churchill

Love helps to purify ourselves from within

True love takes root in your heart when you purify it by getting rid of negative emotions such as anger, greed, jealousy and lust. When you remove these emotions, you create space for receiving the universe's positive flow. This is possible through good deeds and the practice of forgiveness.

The Power of Love brings truth, beauty, energy, knowledge, freedom, goodness and happiness along with it. When we have true love around us, negative influences do not have a big effect on us. With unconditional love, you create positive vibes that dissolve negativity. You enhance the Power of Love in your heart when you stop comparing and start aligning yourself with the Cycle of Creation.

> *It is for this purpose we are born: to love and to be loved.*
> —Mother Teresa

Love helps enhance our focus

Love increases our focus towards constructive thoughts, helps us to have faith in our goals, increases our imagination and inner strength. It is a creative and sustaining energy. It is infinite like the stars in the sky.

Love has magnetic and miraculous powers, and these powers exist beyond matter and energy. It helps us to focus our energies on the work in hand, generating a great power. It is nearly impossible to achieve something unless diversified energies are brought together at a place, leading to creation.

Each one of us is like the earth's calm surface and deep within us are hidden powers that have the potential to explode. These powers can come out only when they are brought together and allowed an outlet. The volcano of powers that erupts within helps us to rise and shine.

'You live to do good and to bring happiness to others.'
—Abdu'l-Baha

2. How to develop your Power of Love

Unconditional love, once expressed, sets in motion a great ripple that has a multiplying affect. The Power of Love makes us a beacon emitting constant light and showing the right direction to others. All good things come back to you. Whenever you send out something without expecting anything in return, it comes back to you sooner or later.

Story: A Glass of Milk

A poor boy used to sell clothes from door to door to pay for his education. One day he realized that he had only ten cents left in his pocket. He was hungry and decided to ask for some food at the next house he went to.

But he lost his hunger when he saw the beautiful young woman who opened the door. Instead of a meal, he asked her for a glass of water. She saw that he was very hungry and brought him a glass of milk. He drank it slowly and then asked, 'How much do I owe you?'

'You do not owe me anything at all,' the woman said. 'My mother taught us never to accept anything for doing someone a kindness'. He replied, 'Then I thank you from the bottom of my heart.'

Years later, the same woman fell gravely ill. The local doctors sent her to the big city where they hoped specialists would be able to make her healthy again.

Dr Howard Kelly was called in as a consultant. When he heard the name of the city where she lived, he got up and went to her room. He immediately recognized her and returned to the consultation room, determined to do his best to save her life. From that day on, he paid special attention to the case. After a long struggle, the battle was finally won.

Dr Kelly left instructions that the bill should be sent to him for authorization. He looked it over, wrote something in the margin and sent it to her room. The woman thought the envelope would contain a bill that would take her the rest of her life to pay in full. But in the margin of the invoice was written, 'Paid in full for a glass of milk: Doctor Howard Kelly.'

Love teaches humility

Love can instil humbleness in you. Through humility you can become a person who is eager to learn, grow and acquire new skills through constant improvement. You must embrace humility if you wish to express the greatness and divinity that lies within you. Modesty can be developed by following a lifestyle of simple living and high thinking. It will help you discover your true nature and qualities such as enthusiasm, wisdom and creativity.

You will realize that there is so much to learn and do in life. Humility instils an urge to be curious and to learn new things. It helps in self-awareness, self-improvement and unlocks the key to greatness. Taking the humble approach means being aware of your weaknesses while developing your strengths.

> *'My religion is simple. My religion is kindness.'*
> —Dalai Lama

Love helps us to let go of our ego

Our ego is the hollow image that we keep associating ourselves with. This hides our true purpose in life. Love has the power to transcend the narrow walls of inflated egos and give us more energy to work. Strength, wisdom, knowledge and skills are bestowed upon us when we give up lust, ego, anger and greed. Anger, arrogance and avarice lead us nowhere. See **Figure 8.1**

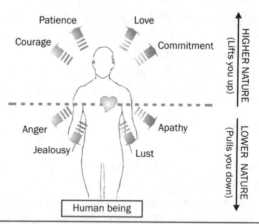

When the human heart focuses on the positive and brighter side of life, man's higher nature develops. This can happen by acquiring spiritual qualities such as love, courage, patience and commitment. On the other hand, if man does not endeavour to develop his higher nature, he is automatically pulled down by the chains of negative attributes such as anger, jealousy, lust and apathy.

THE POWER OF LOVE

FIGURE 8.1

'He who is incapable of hatred towards any being, who is kind and compassionate, free from selfishness . . . Such a devotee of Mine is My beloved.'
—**Bhagavad Gita**

Love helps us to forgive and forget

Forgiveness is the beauty of the soul and is often denied to it. There may be times when people caused you pain. You will often feel hurt and angry. In such cases, you must learn to let go. You will feel relaxed once you forgive someone who wronged you. You will be relieved of past wounds and unconditional love will fill that wound in due course. What is most important here is your decision to forgive and forget.

Forgiveness is unlocking the door to set someone free and realizing you were the person.
—**Max Lucado**

Love makes you observe and not judge others

The Power of Love checks our tendency to judge others. You should also try to get over the negative episodes in your life. Our past mistakes teach us how to get rid of negative emotions.

Love
When a simpleton abused him, Buddha listened to him in silence,
but when the man had finished,
He asked him, 'Son, if a man declined to accept a present offered to him,
to whom would it belong?'
The man answered, 'To him who offered it.'
'My son,' Buddha said, 'I decline to accept your abuse.'
—**Will Durant**

Love can turn enemies into friends

When you start loving yourself and others truly, you will find the world loving you. People will gradually start seeing you in the right manner and begin loving you. All conflicts can be resolved if people talk to each other in a loving and honest way. The Age of Reason is not sufficient for human fulfilment. We must now enter the Age of Love. Forgiveness, compassion and understanding are the core values that must be developed to release the Power of Love.

When you begin each task with love and try to face each situation with love in your heart, you will have no enemies. People see you differently because they have a different opinion about things and have already formed an impression about you. When you change your inside perception, your outside perception changes too. It is like looking at the same coin from different angles.

Someone has rightly said:

'People are often unreasonable, illogical and self-centred;
Forgive them anyway
If you are kind, people may accuse you of selfish,
ulterior motives;
Be kind anyway
If you are successful, you will win some false friends,
and some true enemies;
Succeed anyway.
What you spend years building, someone could
destroy overnight;
Build anyway.
If you find serenity and happiness, they may be jealous,
Be happy anyway.

The good you do today, people will often forget tomorrow;
Do good anyway.
Give the world the best you have, and it may never be
enough;
Give the best anyway.'

Love helps you to look at the best in people

'A man sees in the world what he carries in his heart.'
—**Excerpt from Goethe's** *Faust*

Through the Power of Love, you can learn to appreciate
the inner goodness of every human being. Once you realize
that everyone is truly beautiful from within, you will start
caring about the happiness of other people too.

Abdul Baha rightly said, *'To look always at the good and
not at the bad. If a man has ten good qualities and one bad
one, we must look at the ten and forget the one. And if a man
has ten bad qualities, and one good one, we must look at the
one and forget the ten.'* In the beginning it will be difficult
but as you start following this teaching and start looking at
only the positive aspects of others, you will discover that it
can work miracles.

*'The greatest good you can do for another is not just
share your riches, but to reveal to him his own.'*
—**Benjamin Disraeli**

Love and the deep bond of emotions

Love is essentially pure and unconditional. Just like water
takes on the shape of the vessel in which it is poured, love
takes the form of the kind of heart it is poured in.

Consider the stages of human development and the kind of love relations we share:

When you are a child, you shower your parents, grandparents and siblings with love. When you are an adolescent, you heap love on your friends. On reaching adulthood, you lavish love on your partner or spouse. When you become a parent, you love your children. As you grow old and your children become parents, your love grows for your grandchildren and your grandchildren shower you with love. Love continues to touch our lives with warmth in a cyclic way.

Stage of development	*Love-relationship chart*
Childhood	Love for parents, grandparents and siblings
Adolescence	Love for friends
Adulthood	Love for partner or spouse
Parenthood	Love for children
Old age	Love for grandchildren

If you look carefully, you will find that love remains pure, but the way you express it changes at different stages of your personal growth. Love grows exponentially and its intensity varies at different stages. Just like water may change from solid to liquid or to steam, our love may differ in intensity at different stages of our physical, emotional and spiritual development.

'Great relationships are not necessarily about finding similarities.
Sometimes it is more about respecting differences.'

As you unleash the Power of Love from within, your heart will expand to encompass the whole world.

Treat people well

With the Power of Love in your heart, you must take care to treat people the way you like to be treated yourself. This golden rule can make heaven possible on earth. When you treat people with regard, respect and love, you feel better about yourself.

> 'Some things we keep—
> like a best friend who moved away
> or a classmate we grew up with.
> There are just some things that
> make us happy, no matter what.
> Life is important, and so are the people we know.
> And so, keep them close!'
> —Extract from the poem 'Keep Them Close'
> Author unknown

Loving humanity

Till about a century ago, people could travel without a passport or visa anywhere in the world, without any restriction. National boundaries barely existed. After the two World Wars, many nations started feeling insecure, an identity crisis was triggered and narrow nationalistic feelings became stronger. These feelings became so intense that children were taught to take pride only in their nation's culture and traditions, and the idea of 'national patriotism' took root. This, among other things, widened the divide between the rich and poor across the world.

But in the 21st century the pace of multicultural social and corporate exchanges has quickened once again. And no matter where you are or what you do, you must try to embrace everyone around you in the blanket of unconditional love.

'If you love the world and help people, God will protect you wherever you go.'

—Mokichi Okada

3. An empowering exercise to unleash the Power of Love within you

Visualize the entire universe as a big lake with you standing at its centre. You perceive tranquillity everywhere and the water around you is still. Imagine for a while that there are no emotions and you drop the emotion of love as a pebble from where you stand.

You see the ripples of love surging and spreading in circles around you. The centre is you; the first circle is your family; the next your neighbours, friends and relatives; then your fellow countrymen; and then all the world's citizens. This way the circles reach all across the Earth, encompassing all beings that inhabit this planet.

This exercise will help you to send a ripple of love that will encircle the universe and bring back the ripple of universal and unconditional love towards you, thus empowering you with the Power of Love. **See Figure 8.2**

4. The powerful symbol of love

Water: Water is chosen as the symbol of love because it reflects purity. Water is a life-giving force and takes the shape of the vessel into which it is poured. Pure and unconditional love is also like that. Just as a single drop of water can start a wave, it takes one expression of love to awaken the Power of Love from within, which can stretch to infinity. **See Figure 8.3**

You must widen your Circle of Compassion to embrace all creatures in the universe.

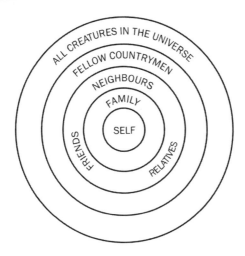

FIGURE 8.2

The symbol of the Power of Love

Water

FIGURE 8.3

5. An empowering personality

How the Power of Love inspired Mother Teresa to heal people and become a messiah of the poorest of the poor

Mother Teresa was born Agnes Gonxha Bojaxhiu in Skopje, Macedonia, on 26 August 1910. At the age of twelve, she felt the call from within to arise and serve humanity. At the age of eighteen she left her parental home and joined the Sisters of Loreto, an Irish community of nuns with missions in India.

While teaching at St Mary's High School in Calcutta, the glimpse of suffering and poverty outside the convent walls made a deep impression on her. In 1948 she received permission from her superiors to leave the convent school and devote herself to working among the poorest of the poor in the slums of Calcutta. This was a life-transforming decision in Mother Teresa's life. Through her initiative and dynamic leadership the Missionaries of Charity came to existence. The organization's primary task was to love and care for the poor, the sick and the deprived. Mother Teresa said, 'If you can't feed a hundred people, then feed just one.'

Her work for the poor was greatly appreciated and supported by the world community. People started seeing her as an angel of love. In 1979 she was awarded the Nobel Prize in Peace. 'There is so much suffering, so much hatred, so much misery, and we with our prayer, with our sacrifice are beginning at home,' she said in her Nobel Lecture. 'Love begins at home, and it is not how much we do, but how much love we put in the action that we do.'

Because of her commitment and zeal to reach the poor and needy, by 1990 the Missionaries of Charity had over one million volunteers in more than 40 countries. Mother Teresa continued to serve and heal people till her death in 1997. The Power of Love gave her the courage to keep going on.

Three important lessons can be learnt from Mother Teresa's life.

1) '*If you judge people, you can't love them.*' Rather than judge people and expect them to be 'the way we want', we should accept them 'as they are'.

2) '*Every time you smile at someone, it is an action of love, a gift to that person, a beautiful thing.*' Smile at people every time you greet them. You will find people smiling back in return.

3) Speak politely with everyone, no matter who that person is.

6. EIGHT EMPOWERING QUESTIONS

i. Can I add joy and happiness to the people I meet today by having a smile on my face?

ii. What are the two unique things that are good about me? How can I use them for the maximum benefit of all?

iii. What is one thing that I would love to do most of the time?

iv. How can I inspire someone so that they perform better? How can I help them?

v. Am I creating time and space to do something today that I really love to do? What new things am I learning today?

vi. Have I forgiven those who have done me wrong? Have I forgiven myself?

vii. Do I love everyone and everything unconditionally and impartially, including those who do not love me?

viii. How can I expand my circle of love daily?

7. Eight empowering affirmations

i. When I smile at people I meet, they smile back. This positive response gives me joy and happiness.

ii. I feel proud of the unique gifts bestowed upon me and I use them to empower myself and others.

iii. Love is helping me grow and I am doing the most productive thing possible at every given moment.

iv. Every day I am becoming worthy of the love of others. I praise others and feel happy about inspiring them.

v. Every day I am accepting life as an incredible miracle with love in my heart. I am thankful for the gift of each new day.

vi. I have plenty of time to do the things I want to do. I am able to learn and do what I want to do.

vii. I am able to induce positive feelings in the people I meet and I've dissolved and released all jealousy from my heart.

viii. I forgive myself and others easily.

8. Eight tips to help you enhance your power of love

1) **Learn to give without expectations.** Whenever you offer any help to a stranger, do it without any expectation in

return. There is nothing more valuable than a kind act and when you perform it with unconditional love, a sense of joy will pervade through your being.

2) **Be an observer and do not judge people or situations.** When you are in an awkward situation, try not judge the situation or the people involved in it. Be open and try to observe the situation as it is and not as you want to see it.

3) **Make others feel good about themselves.** Try to know people and their good qualities. An honest appreciation of their qualities will make them feel good. Someone has rightly said, 'People may not remember exactly what you did, or what you said, but they will always remember how you made them feel.'

4) **Use the Power of Love to unite hearts.** If you work as part of a team, you should use the Power of Love to unite people. Love, a powerful unifying force, is the very foundation of strong teamwork. When one gives or receives unconditional love with pure intentions, the hearts of the giver and the receiver are united as one. This unity of heart creates a unity of vision, purpose and action.

5) **Develop a positive attitude with love in your heart.** When you have genuine love in your heart, you start adopting a positive attitude in your behaviour. The Power of Love helps you to wipe out negative emotions from your heart and look forward with a positive attitude towards every event in your life.

6) **The Power of Love enhances your focus.** With little or no negative emotions in your heart, you are able to focus

better on achieving your goals. The Power of Love acts like a converging lens that brings your energies together and concentrates your strength to take positive action.

7) **The Power of Love unlocks your creativity.** Once you are loving, focused and have a positive attitude, your creativity is unlocked. You will then use your time to do creative things. And a creative mind is evidence of love in the heart.

8) **You can develop an attitude of gratitude:** Through the Power of Love you can develop an attitude of thankfulness. With the flow of love in your heart, you become thankful for the various gifts that life has bestowed upon you. By being grateful, you will invite more and more good things in your life.

Success Principle #8:
Use the Power of Love

Remember that love is the strongest power. Love binds us and connects us all. Enlarge your heart and your circle of love: love yourself, your family, your neighbours, those who do not like you, your fellow countrymen, all the citizens of the world and all life on Earth. Love everyone, and one day you will find everyone loving you. Begin now.

The Eight Success Principles

All the 'infinite success' principles are interdependent and should be applied in unison to get the desired result.

SUCCESS PRINCIPLE #1: USE THE POWER OF IMAGINATION

Visualize what you want to achieve and create a strong mental image of your goals. Hold these images till you make them come true.

SUCCESS PRINCIPLE #2: USE THE POWER OF WORDS

Think, speak, read, write and listen to only positive, beautiful and affirmative words (as far as possible). The words that touch you in any form affect you strongly and shape your thoughts, attitudes and character—the three foundations of success.

SUCCESS PRINCIPLE #3: USE THE POWER OF SELF-CONFIDENCE

Have full confidence in your powers. Keep telling yourself that your future will evolve just the way you want it to—and that this will happen sooner rather than later.

SUCCESS PRINCIPLE#4: USE THE POWER OF GOAL SETTING

Set your goals in the direction of what you want and love to do the most. Keep the burning desire alive in your heart and act with a calm mind.

SUCCESS PRINCIPLE #5: USE THE POWER OF FOCUS

Focus on what you want and on doing one thing at a time. The more you are able to focus on a task, the better you become and your chances of success increase.

SUCCESS PRINCIPLE #6: USE THE POWER OF WILL

Develop your willpower by using self-determination and self-discipline to keep a check over your negative emotions, and do what is necessary.

SUCCESS PRINCIPLE #7: USE THE POWER OF ACTION

Do most of the time what you would like to do the most. Stick with steadfastness to your goals and take constant action to accomplish them, come what may. Also take out time to assess 'where you are from' and 'where you have to go'.

SUCCESS PRINCIPLE #8: USE THE POWER OF LOVE

Remember that love is the strongest power. Love binds us and connects us all. Enlarge your heart and your circle of love: love yourself, your family, your neighbours, those who do not like you, your fellow countrymen, all the citizens of the world and all life on Earth. Love everyone, and one day you will find everyone loving you. Begin now.

The Eight Lessons of Life

There was a small village by the sea. The villagers lived a simple and peaceful life. But one thing aroused their curiosity: a shining island in the sea. People had talked about the island for many generations, but no one had dared to visit it.

One day two friends, Peter and Henry, decided to set sail to the deserted island.

Their plan was to row to the island at night—when there would be few people watching them—and return in the morning.

Life's Lesson#1: Dream, aim, plan and work

At night they started on their journey. They rowed all night. But next morning they discovered that they were still where they had started.

Why?

Because they had forgotten to pull the anchor.

Life's Lesson #2: Know what is holding you back and get rid of it.

Remember to remove the obstacles which have been holding you back. Get rid of them before you start.

Peter and Henry did not give up. They pulled up the anchor and started to row. Again they spent the night rowing hard. But morning came and they were still where they had started.

Why?

Because they were rowing in opposite directions. The boat simply didn't move ahead.

Life's Lesson #3: When you work with a partner, make sure you both work in the same direction.

Team effort should be coordinated in such a way that work progresses in the right direction.

The third night Peter and Henry decided to row again. They pulled up the anchor and rowed together. But they were still stuck at the same place the next morning.

Reason?

They didn't bother to change the direction of the rudder. So they kept circling the same spot.

Life's Lesson #4: Make sure you know exactly where you are going and channel your direction accordingly.

Constantly monitor the direction of your efforts. Otherwise you may remain at the same spot.

Peter and Henry were now exhausted. They went to an old man in their village for advice. The old man told them that night wasn't the right time to sail because of the current. To reduce their chances of making a mistake, they must sail during the day. The two friends decided to follow the advice.

Life's Lesson #5: Seek guidance from someone who has knowledge and experience of the planned task.

Next morning, Peter and Henry removed the anchor, rowed together and kept an eye on the rudder. The boat moved smoothly ahead.

After they saw a fishing boat, Henry suggested, 'Peter, what if we don't find anything to eat on the island? Wouldn't it be a good idea to go fishing first?'

'You are right,' said Peter. 'But there is a small problem. We are halfway through and we don't have a fishing net. Maybe we can borrow one from the vessel ahead.'

Life's Lesson #6: Be flexible in the process of achieving goals.

You can change your goal at the start but not in the middle of the journey. So, show flexibility if you face an unexpected situation.

Later, Peter and Henry saw a big shark with her mouth open, waiting to engulf them. Henry jumped off the boat, found refuge on a passing ship and returned to the village.

Peter kept his cool. He took the oar Henry had left behind and pushed it in the open mouth of the shark when it came near him. The shark swam away.

Life's Lesson #7: Face the problem and look for a solution straightaway.

While approaching your goal, you will face many challenges. Running away won't help. The solution to the problem is always near the problem. If you stay calm and use your head, you will be able to overcome all challenges.

Peter kept rowing towards the island. After a couple of hours, he reached his destination. He took a round of the island and found that it was barren. No trace of life or riches was there. But he spotted some shining stones which glittered during the day. These were the stones that made the island shine.

Peter was sad and thought his trip had not been worthwhile. While leaving the island, he picked up some coloured stones for his children to play with. He reached home that same evening. His children liked the sparkling stones he got for them and started playing with them. Peter was satisfied that he had at least attained his goal of going to the island and returning.

A month later, a jeweller from the village came up to Peter and asked him if he was willing to sell the stones for a huge sum. 'Why?' said the surprised sailor. 'Because they are diamonds,' replied the jeweller. Peter was happy for he realized just what he had discovered.

Life's Lesson #8: Be happy when you achieve your goal and collect the gifts it brings—even if they are stones.

Even if you reach your goal and find nothing but stones there, be happy for two reasons: you have reached your goal and have found something new.

Epilogue

Life is too tough if we take our powers for granted and do not make full use of them. Life can be smooth if we use our powers effectively and apply them well. The eight powers within you, if used in harmony with the laws of the universe, can make a huge difference to your life. I have tested and applied these powers in my own life and found amazing results. If you work to develop these powers from within, you too will get remarkable results. **See Figure E1**

You are born to be great

The seed of greatness lies within you and you are born to express this greatness. It is hard to look at a seed and correctly predict the height of the tree it will one day grow into and the quality of fruits it will bear. Look at the situation again. Today you might be able to hold the seed in your palm, but one day you might not be able to encircle it even with both hands. This is true of humans too. As Shakespeare said, 'You may know what you are, but you don't know what you can be.'

FIGURE E1

Think big. Dream more. Think of infinite possibilities—where you can be and what you can create. You will soon find yourself doing what is possible, and with more effort you will find yourself doing what seemed to be impossible at one time.

Empower others as you get empowered

Once you have understood and developed the concept of success, share it with others. You may be tempted to keep the secret of success to yourself, but what is the point of being lonely at the top?

A good way to express your powers is to empower others through your positive words and deeds. At the same time, avoid using words that dispirit people and reduce their energy level. Express honest appreciation of people and be grateful to them for any kind deed they do to you. People like being given attention and you must endeavour to do so.

It's the journey that's important

'Life, sometimes so wearying
Is worth its weight in gold
The experience of travelling
Lends a wisdom that is old
Beyond our "living memory"
A softly spoken prayer:
"It's the journey that's important,
Not the getting there!"'

—John McLeod

Self-improvement and the world

The process of working towards attaining your goals will bring out a marked change in you. Next, you should extend yourself and work to bring about a positive change in the lives of others too. Why not bring about a change in the world? Why not take the initiative to lead and change?

The 20th century saw a great advance in the self-improvement campaign across the world. From Napolean Hill and Dale Carnegie in the 1930s to present-day self-growth gurus such as Anthony Robbins, Deepak Chopra and Zig

Ziglar, hundreds of experts, books, audio and video tapes offered advice on bringing out the best in us.

In the 21st century, people feel a new connectedness to each other—even while sitting thousands of miles apart, they can stay in touch with the aid of various means of communication. This makes them realize that there is no fun in growing individually alone. While the richer nations and their people become richer, over a billion people still survive on less than a dollar a day. No wonder, informed individuals feel the need to do something for the wider world. In the age of communication, the pain of disasters such as the 2004 India Ocean tsunami and big earthquakes is felt by people everywhere.

People are interested in self-growth, but they realize that the world—the one next door and the one beyond—too must see sustainable growth. They want to grow personally and also help others grow.

If you look at **Figure E2**, it will help you explore the eight directions in which you can grow.

With this approach, the holistic growth of individuals as well as humanity will not seem impossible to achieve. It will lead to a new age of 'collective-growth' based on love and cooperation. It will be a win-win situation.

Humanity has always hoped for some miracle that will lead this divided and unequal world into an era of love, unity and equality. The good news: the emerging new world order is already visible. Unlike the slow progress made from ancient times till a couple of centuries ago, vast changes are now being made in a short span of time. Things will not change overnight, but they will.

Before I close, I would like to remind the reader that this

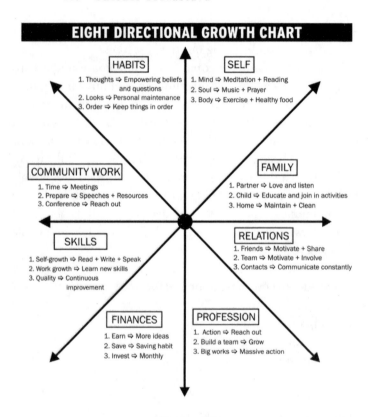

EIGHT DIRECTIONAL GROWTH CHART

HABITS
1. Thoughts ⇨ Empowering beliefs and questions
2. Looks ⇨ Personal maintenance
3. Order ⇨ Keep things in order

SELF
1. Mind ⇨ Meditation + Reading
2. Soul ⇨ Music + Prayer
3. Body ⇨ Exercise + Healthy food

COMMUNITY WORK
1. Time ⇨ Meetings
2. Prepare ⇨ Speeches + Resources
3. Conference ⇨ Reach out

FAMILY
1. Partner ⇨ Love and listen
2. Child ⇨ Educate and join in activities
3. Home ⇨ Maintain + Clean

SKILLS
1. Self-growth ⇨ Read + Write + Speak
2. Work growth ⇨ Learn new skills
3. Quality ⇨ Continuous improvement

RELATIONS
1. Friends ⇨ Motivate + Share
2. Team ⇨ Motivate + Involve
3. Contacts ⇨ Communicate constantly

FINANCES
1. Earn ⇨ More ideas
2. Save ⇨ Saving habit
3. Invest ⇨ Monthly

PROFESSION
1. Action ⇨ Reach out
2. Build a team ⇨ Grow
3. Big works ⇨ Massive action

FIGURE E2

is just the beginning of your journey to discover your hidden potential through the eight powers within you. I hope you have found this book useful and will use these powers in the best interest of the whole world.

Contact the author

Visit www.eightpowers.com for more details about this book. Readers are invited to share their stories and experiences regarding the eight powers within. Interesting accounts will be posted on the website.

The author can be reached at book@eightpowers.com.